Daily
Prayers
and
Promises
for
Women

To Audrey

Daily Prayers and Promises for Women

Love from
Gwynnett
xoxo

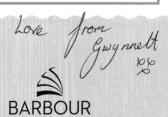

BARBOUR
PUBLISHING

© 2003 by Barbour Publishing, Inc.

Compiled by Hope Clarke.

ISBN 978-1-64352-849-6

Selections included are taken from *Prayers & Promises* by Toni Sortor and Pamela McQuade, © 2001 by Barbour Publishing, Inc.; *Prayers & Promises for Women* by Toni Sortor, © 2003 by Barbour Publishing, Inc.; *Prayers & Promises for Men* by John Hudson Tiner, © 2003 by Barbour Publishing, Inc.; and *Prayers & Promises for the Graduate* by Pamela McQuade, © 2003 by Barbour Publishing, Inc.

Published by Barbour Publishing, Inc., 1810 Barbour Drive, Uhrichsville, Ohio 44683, www.barbourbooks.com

Our mission is to inspire the world with the life-changing message of the Bible.

Member of the
Evangelical Christian
Publishers Association

Printed in China.

Day 1
A To-Do List Christian

*To every thing there is a season, and a time
to every purpose under the heaven.*
ECCLESIASTES 3:1

I am a to-do list person, Lord. The multitude
of those activities threatens to spill into the
time I have set aside for prayer. I've moved
prayer to category one—an absolutely, pos-
itively, must-do activity. Forgive me when
taking time to talk to You does not come automatically and naturally.

Father, You'll notice the pad of paper at my
side as I come to You in prayer. When unfinished
items intrude on my mind, I'll write them down
and set them aside so that I can concentrate on
talking with You. I am thankful that we have this
time to spend together.

Day 2
Peace

When a man's ways please the LORD,
he maketh even his enemies
to be at peace with him.
PROVERBS 16:7

Lord, You know I want my ways to please You. Serving You is the greatest thing I can do with my life. As an added benefit, You have promised that because I obey, You will smooth my path. Even my enemies will become peaceful.

I've already seen Your promise at work in my life. Sometimes, when life seems to be getting rough, I pray—and the path becomes smooth before me. Issues I thought would become real problems turn into nothing at all, and I know You have answered my prayer.

Thank You for Your peace, which goes before me every day to bless my life.

Day 3
God's Giving

"But seek first his kingdom and his
righteousness, and all these things
will be given to you as well."
MATTHEW 6:33 NIV

I'd like to have You give me all kinds of nice things in life, Lord. Good food and drink and nice clothes would be a good place to start. . .a nice place to live would be great. . . . Before long, I have a long list of wants.

But those aren't the things You really want me to desire. They're just the "extras." What You want me to seek first is Your kingdom and righteousness. You want me to want what You want and be what You are.

You give me so many good things, Lord. Help me to understand the source of every blessing and rejoice in You alone. Help me to live to rejoice in You—not the things You give.

Day 4
Never Alone

I am a companion of all them that fear thee,
and of them that keep thy precepts.
PSALM 119:63

I know a church that refuses to give in to fear, Lord. Its doors are never locked, and sometimes I go in on my way home, sit alone in a pew, and enjoy the shadowed quiet. When I go to services there on Sunday, the church is full and no one needs to be lonely. The congregation welcomes me with brotherly love.

But I relish my early evening visits with You, for although I may be alone in the sanctuary, I feel the presence of two thousand years of saints—brothers and sisters You love and still call by name. Because of You I am never lonely. My roots are deep; Your family of faith is always with me.

Day 5
The Fruit of Righteousness

Say ye to the righteous, that it shall be well with him: for they shall eat the fruit of their doings.

ISAIAH 3:10

I do Your work expecting no material reward, Father. Those I help often have nothing to give in return; and if they did, I would not want to take it from their families. My reward comes from the giving itself; and even when the giving can be painful, I continue for Your sake.

Although I ask nothing for my acts of conscience, You are quick to bless me. When I give honesty, I am treated honestly. When I give love, I am loved. When I provide justice, others are just with me. When I ask for nothing, You give me everything I could ever hope for and will never deserve.

Day 6
God's Direction

"Anyone who sets aside one of the least of these commands and teaches others accordingly will be called least in the kingdom of heaven, but whoever practices and teaches these commands will be called great in the kingdom of heaven."
MATTHEW 5:19 NIV

You've given me a choice, Lord: to obey or break Your commandments. And You've told me the outcome of each.

Sometimes Your commandments aren't easy to understand, but I want to learn all about them and obey them more and more each day. You've given them to guide me in the right direction and keep me from messing up my life. Thank You for caring where I go and what I do, Father.

Help me to obey and pass on Your commands to others who also need Your direction in their lives. Without Your commands, we'd all be going in circles, Lord.

Day 7
Overcoming Fear

Watch ye, stand fast in the faith,
quit you like men, be strong.
1 CORINTHIANS 16:13

Father, I pray that I can overcome fears that hinder me from following in Your footsteps. Fear makes me a liar: I excuse myself by claiming that I don't know how or that I'm not ready. Fear makes me a pretender: I can be fainthearted or hesitant, and I call it patience.

Regardless of the nature of my anxiety, I must press ahead. Lord, may I embrace Your Word in order to drive out irrational concerns that trouble my heart. I pray that I will not allow fear to paralyze me.

Day 8
Bright Spots of Light

How then shall they call on him in whom they have not believed? and how shall they believe in him of whom they have not heard? and how shall they hear without a preacher?

ROMANS 10:14

Father, I ask that You watch over my leaders today and all the days to come. They have accepted a responsibility that few would ever accept: the care for the souls of others. I know the work is demanding, for I add my own demands to those of others. I know the outward rewards are few, for our budgets are limited. Yet still they carry on, bright spots shining in the midst of dark humanity.

Wherever possible, make their loads lighter; where that is impossible, make their shoulders strong. Be with them throughout the long days and sleepless nights, and assure them that their work is not in vain.

Day 9
Real Dangers

Wherefore gird up the loins of your mind,
be sober, and hope to the end for the grace
that is to be brought unto you at the
revelation of Jesus Christ.

1 PETER 1:13

Sometimes danger is too real. A child becomes dangerously ill, a relative has a stroke, or someone we love is in an accident. We all react differently to such disasters, but eventually we all fall apart. Even those who seem strong as a rock shake on the inside. Somehow we manage to cope, to hold ourselves together and do what needs to be done in spite of our fear and grief. We live in hope: first in hope of a cure, then, if that fails, in hope of salvation. When all hope seems to be lost, Lord, be with those who suffer. Help them to never abandon hope, for all things are possible with You.

Day 10
God Owns All Creation

The earth is the LORD's, and everything in it.
The world and all its people belong to him.
PSALM 24:1 NLT

Thank You, Lord, for controlling all creation, though things can seem so confused. I often wonder where this world is going, but I'm glad I can trust in Your control over all living things.

Even people, whom You created along with the birds, bees, and other creatures, are under Your control. Though they may not all glorify You with their lives, they cannot do anything to set aside Your command of creation. Their wickedness cannot destroy Your plans for Your world.

Thank You for owning me, along with everything else. I'm incredibly glad to belong to the Lord of the universe.

Day 11
No Free Lunch

For by grace are ye saved through faith;
and that not of yourselves: it is the gift of God:
not of works, lest any man should boast.
EPHESIANS 2:8–9

Lord, because I have heard the statement "There is no such thing as a free lunch," so often I view with skepticism anything that is offered for free. Even accepting Your grace is difficult. But You have overcome my reluctance by showing that although grace is free to me, it did come at a price. If I do not accept Your grace, then Jesus' death for me was in vain.

Father, I have become a privileged child, receiving favors and divine protection merely by accepting Your gift of salvation. You have delivered me from the captivity of sin and restored me to a life of freedom. Thank You, Lord.

Day 12
Humble Prayer

When he maketh inquisition for blood,
he remembereth them: he forgetteth
not the cry of the humble.

PSALM 9:12

How many times, Lord, have I wondered if You heard my prayers? When wickedness surrounds me and You don't seem to act, I blame the entire world or begin to think Your ears are closed.

If pride has caused my troubles, show me where it lies in me, Holy One. Humble my heart before You so I can admit my guilt.

But if I must simply await Your moment for justice, let humility bring patient expectation that You will remember and act. You hear every breath of my cries when I obey You.

Day 13
Hidden Strength

*He gives strength to the weary
and increases the power of the weak.*
ISAIAH 40:29 NIV

I am not courageous, Lord. Like a child, sometimes I still wonder about the monsters under the bed and turn on every light in the house as soon as the sun sets. When I look at my life's challenges, I feel so small and inadequate.

Yet You promise courage and strength when I need them. Sometimes, in Your power, I even do remarkable things that cannot be explained; I can rise to great heights when necessary. After the danger is passed, my knees may give out, and I wonder how I did such wonders. Then the light dawns: You did wonders through me. Thank You for the hidden strength You give me—Your strength.

Day 14
In the Midst of Trouble

Though I walk in the midst of trouble,
thou wilt revive me: thou shalt stretch forth
thine hand against the wrath of mine enemies,
and thy right hand shall save me.
PSALM 138:7

We all seem to be walking in the midst of trouble these days, Lord. Suddenly we have enemies we never knew were enemies, people who prefer deception and violence to diplomacy. We do not understand them, and they misunderstand us. We are a hurt nation—an angry nation struggling to maintain its values while still dealing firmly with those who hate us. Guide our nation's leaders during these difficult times, we pray. Keep our sons and daughters safe in Your arms. Bring peace and security back into this hurting world for all so we may learn the lessons of this conflict and live together in harmony.

Day 15
A Living Stone

Ye also, as lively stones, are built up a spiritual house, an holy priesthood, to offer up spiritual sacrifices, acceptable to God by Jesus Christ.
1 PETER 2:5

Lord, I am amazed at the ceaseless action of waves. I find stones that are rounded smooth by the continuous pounding of the water. Even the edges of broken glass are smoothed away until they are no longer sharp.

Father, I see Your ceaseless action on my life in the same way. Day by day, You remove my rough edges. You blunt my sharp tongue, soften my overbearing manner, cool my hot temper, and smooth out my uneven disposition. From a rough and unremarkable stone, You have made me into something better. Thank You for continuously changing me.

Day 16
Wholehearted Service

*"No one can serve two masters. For you
will hate one and love the other; you will be
devoted to one and despise the other. You
cannot serve God and be enslaved to money."*
LUKE 16:13 NLT

Many desirable things quickly turn me from You,
Lord. I admit I willingly fall far from You when
worldly toys attract me. Forgive me for placing
anything ahead of Your love.

Though deep down I know things can never
replace You, when money or goods attract me, I
don't usually ponder the exchange I'd be making. I want to believe I can have it all. Remind me,
Lord, that to be faithful to You, even my money
must serve You. Spiritual things have so much
more value than the wealth I desire.

Make me wholeheartedly desire Your will,
Jesus, so I cannot serve the wrong master.

TUES.

Day 17
Avoiding Doubt

Jesus replied, "Truly I tell you, if you have faith and do not doubt, not only can you do what was done to the fig tree, but also you can say to this mountain, 'Go, throw yourself into the sea,' and it will be done."

MATTHEW 21:21 NIV

It's hard for me to imagine this kind of faith, Lord. So often my own seems to get stuck under mountains instead of moving them. But I know that if You promise such things, they can happen.

Remove my doubt, O Lord. As I trust more fully in You, I know my faith will become strong enough to do Your will. That may not include mountain moving, but I know it can change lives, bring hope, and draw others to You.

Actually, you might call that moving a mountain after all!

Day 18
A Lively Hope

*Blessed be the God and Father of our
Lord Jesus Christ, which according
to his abundant mercy hath begotten
us again unto a lively hope by the
resurrection of Jesus Christ from the dead.*

1 PETER 1:3

I know that hope comes in many forms, Father. There is grudging hope, reluctant hope, tentative hope, even doubtful hope. It is, after all, in my nature to hope, even when hope has failed me before and will surely do so again.

But You, through the resurrection of Your Son, Jesus Christ, offer me a "lively" hope, a hope that never disappoints or fails. When my human hopes turn to dust, Your promise abides: "For God so loved the world, that he gave his only begotten Son, that whosoever believeth in him should not perish, but have everlasting life" (John 3:16).

Day 19
Becoming Wise

Thou hast known the holy scriptures, which are able to make thee wise unto salvation through faith which is in Christ Jesus. All scripture is given by inspiration of God, and is profitable for doctrine, for reproof, for correction, for instruction in righteousness.

2 TIMOTHY 3:15–16

You offer me so much wisdom in Your Book, Lord. Not only have You used it to draw me to Your side in salvation, You provide me with a lifetime of insight for leading a life that glorifies You and makes me more like You.

I praise You for Your generous sharing of Yourself. Though I will never be as wise as You, knowing all things, You have graciously shared this part of Your nature. I am blessed by Your touch. May I live every moment by the light of Your Word and become righteous through knowledge of Your Son, Jesus Christ.

Day 20
God's Direction

*Trust in the LORD with all thine
heart; and lean not unto thine own
understanding. In all thy ways acknowledge
him, and he shall direct thy paths.*
PROVERBS 3:5–6

I never know what the day will bring, Lord. A perfectly ordinary day may end with glory or grief, or it may end like a perfectly ordinary day usually ends. I try to prepare myself for anything that comes my way, at least mentally; but the truth is, there are too many possibilities for me to even consider. All I can do is put my trust in You and live each day in the belief that You know how everything will work out—even if I don't. You will show me which way to turn. You will guide and protect me day after day. You have a plan; and although I don't know or understand it, I trust in You.

Day 21
A Nice, Sunny Spot

*And he shall be like a tree planted by the
rivers of water, that bringeth forth his fruit
in his season; his leaf also shall not wither;
and whatsoever he doeth shall prosper.*

PSALM 1:3

If I were a fruit tree, I would want to be planted
in a nice, sunny spot by a river. That would take
care of my strongest needs—sunlight and water.
Other trees planted in the shade or a dry field
would have a harder time, and their fruits
would not be as good as mine. Where we are
planted makes a big difference.

I am planted in You, Lord. I will take care to
keep my roots strong in You. I will have patience,
knowing my season is coming according to
Your timetable and trusting that with Your help,
every fruit I produce will be good.

Day 22
The End

*For God so loved the world, that he gave
his only begotten Son, that whosoever
believeth in him should not perish,
but have everlasting life.*
JOHN 3:16

Father, I avoid reading movie or book reviews that go into too much detail about the plot. I enjoy the suspense of waiting to learn how the story unfolds. The ending may be happy or it may have a twist, but I want to be surprised by it.

However, in my own life, I want to know the final result. Thank You, Lord, for telling me the outcome. You have promised that if I seek You, I will find You. Jesus has already paid the penalty for my sins. A faithful life assures me that I will have an eternal home with You.

Day 23
Making Decisions

Have not I commanded thee? Be strong and of a good courage; be not afraid, neither be thou dismayed: for the LORD thy God is with thee whithersoever thou goest.

JOSHUA 1:9

Lord, I often must make decisions on short notice that affect me and others. Despite complex situations, I must answer with a yes or no and do it quickly. The proper course of action is not always obvious because I may lack all the facts necessary to make a well-informed decision. Yet, I cannot delay because the decision must be made today, not tomorrow.

Dear Jesus, I always want my choices to be in keeping with the examples set by You. But when the options appear equally valid, each having risks and benefits, I pray I will be both wise and decisive.

Day 24
Forgiving Love

*"Don't tear your clothing in your grief,
but tear your hearts instead." Return to
the* LORD *your God, for he is merciful and
compassionate, slow to get angry and
filled with unfailing love. He is eager
to relent and not punish.*

JOEL 2:13 NLT

When I've done wrong, it's comforting to know You want me to return to You, Lord. Though it seems right that You should hold my sin against me, that's not Your desire. You've already forgiven my sin with Jesus' sacrifice. I need simply to turn to You and acknowledge my unfaithfulness.

Turn my heart from wrongdoing, Lord. I don't want to miss out on a moment of Your love and grace. Draw me close, Jesus, to Your wounded side, where I can rejoice in Your forgiving love.

Day 25
Following Jesus

"Whoever serves me must follow me;
and where I am, my servant also will be.
My Father will honor the one who serves me."
JOHN 12:26 NIV

Jesus, I want to be where You are, not miles away trying to fulfill my own needs. Instead of seeking my own path, I must listen to Your call on my life and put Your commands into action. I must hear Your Word each day and listen to Your still, small voice as it speaks to my heart.

If I follow closely, You promise that Your Father will honor me. Though that honor can't be my only reason for obeying You, I'm thankful for the rewards my obedience will earn. I need the blessings You offer, Lord.

Day 26
Glorifying God

*But he that glorieth, let him
glory in the Lord. For not he that
commendeth himself is approved,
but whom the Lord commendeth.*
2 Corinthians 10:17–18

I can't look good in Your eyes, Lord, by glorifying myself. When I try to do that, I only become self-righteous. Forgive me for my tendency to put myself ahead of You. But thank You that I can glory in Your righteousness. How wonderful are Your moral laws and the commendation You give when I do Your will.

May I only seek to lift You up, Lord. May my words tell of Your goodness instead of my own. When I hear Your words of commendation, they will still only reflect Your glory.

Day 27
Good News

Therefore my people shall know my name: therefore they shall know in that day that I am he that doth speak: behold, it is I. How beautiful upon the mountains are the feet of him that bringeth good tidings, that publisheth peace.

ISAIAH 52:6–7

How glad I am, Lord, that You sent me a messenger with the Good News so that I could have peace with You. Whether it was a trained evangelist or a hometown missionary who spoke across the coffee cups, that person brought precious news.

Bless those who take Your Word to people who have never heard it. Whether Your messengers live in a foreign place or have an outreach within my own church, bless them and their message. May they publish peace to all the world.

Day 28
Meeting Together

The rich and poor meet together:
the LORD is the maker of them all.
PROVERBS 22:2

I refuse to let envy cloud my life, Lord, but sometimes it's hard to feel that I have anything in common with the rich. After all, I could redo my kitchen on what they earn in less than a month. If I were to suddenly become rich, I wouldn't even know what to do with the money left over after my needs were filled. There's really a lot that the rich and poor could learn from each other if they took the time; and maybe they should, because we are all Your children. We have You as our common ancestor, the Creator who loves us all. When envy creeps into my heart, let me be happy for those You have blessed—in any way. There is more than enough of Your love to share.

Day 29
Greatness Redefined

And whosoever shall receive me receiveth him that sent me: for he that is least among you all, the same shall be great.

LUKE 9:48

You continued Your lesson by saying that anyone who welcomes You also welcomes Your Father, who sent You. Social status, education, riches—all the things that society values—are not as important to You as faith, which even the humblest child can possess. This is a difficult concept to teach children today, Lord. Society encourages the worship of sports figures and pop stars, the rich and the famous. I need to redefine "greatness" for my children and show them worthy examples of those who have received You. They need to know that there is a better, more glorious way to live—one so simple that even a young child can understand it.

Day 30
Counting Blessings

Enter into his gates with thanksgiving,
and into his courts with praise: be thankful
unto him, and bless his name.
PSALM 100:4

Dear Lord, what a bountiful harvest I have received from You! I count blessings without number. You have given me health, a warm family life, prosperity, and a peaceful heart. You have given me strength in adversity and security in turmoil. You have given me opportunities to serve and thereby enriched my life.

I acknowledge the rich blessings that You have showered upon me. Help me appreciate them. Remove from my heart the idea that my recognition of these blessings will earn me future blessings. Let me focus on what You have done for me and rejoice in all the daily blessings You give me.

Day 31
Of Praise

His glory covered the heavens,
and the earth was full of his praise.

HABAKKUK 3:3

Almighty Father of all creation, accept this prayer of praise. I respect You, venerate You, and honor You as the Creator of the universe and everything in it. I recognize You as my maker. I am thankful that You were too kind to create the world and then walk away from it. Instead, You take an interest in my daily life and care about my eternal well-being.

I sometimes hesitate to offer praise because doing so implies that I understand enough of Your power to appreciate it. Despite this misgiving, may I always praise You for Your love, the grace of Jesus, and the guidance of the Holy Spirit.

Day 32
Heart's Desires

Trust in the LORD, and do good; dwell in the land, and feed on His faithfulness. Delight yourself also in the LORD, and He shall give you the desires of your heart.
PSALM 37:3–4 NKJV

What a generous Lord You are, Father God, wanting to give me my heart's desires. If I trust and obey You, live in a way that glorifies You, and put You first in my life, my life and heart become full. But whenever I'm less than devoted, no matter how much I receive, my heart remains empty. Only a life focused on You is perfectly blessed.

Though I seek my own desires, they always escape me. They're always one arm's length beyond my grasp—until I live in obedience to You. Then my elusive desires slip within reach because You've blessed my grasp. My desires become Yours, and suddenly I have them.

Day 33
Faith Tested

Count it all joy when you fall into various trials, knowing that the testing of your faith produces patience.
JAMES 1:2–3 NKJV

I don't enjoy having my faith tested, Lord. It can hurt deeply, and I'd avoid many such challenges if I could. But You, knowing what's best for me, don't let me get away with that attitude. Instead You toss me into situations I don't like because they'll make me stronger. As situations or people irritate me and I stand firm, I become more patient.

I'd never think of asking for trials, but without them I'd never be longsuffering with others. I'd never gain Your character, and I wouldn't put up with much.

Thank You for the trials I try to avoid. They've been a blessing to me.

Day 34
My Stewardship

*The LORD shall open unto thee his good
treasure, the heaven to give the rain
unto thy land in his season, and to
bless all the work of thine hand.*

DEUTERONOMY 28:12

Father, the world abounds with Your blessings:
fertile soil, nourishing rain, the warmth of the
sun, the cooling breezes. Everything I need is
given to me as a gift, and I am free to use it all.

You have given me stewardship of this
world, but I have often failed in my responsibilities. I have depleted the soil, fouled the rivers
and seas, polluted the air, and exterminated Your
creatures in my haste to make myself rich. Forgive me these trespasses against Your creation,
Father. Show me where I have done wrong.
Teach me how to correct my selfish acts and live
in harmony with Your precious world. When I
do, that will be the true measure of my success.

Day 35
My Rock

God is not a man, that he should lie; neither the son of man, that he should repent: hath he said, and shall he not do it? or hath he spoken, and shall he not make it good?

NUMBERS 23:19

Father, because I was made in Your image, I sometimes think I can project my own weaknesses back on You, who has no weakness. I lie; I change my mind; I do not always honor my promises. All this is very human, but this is not a reflection of You. I make a grave mistake when I assume my faults are also Your faults.

You do not treat me as I treat others. What You promise, You will fulfill to the last word. What You say You will do, You will do. When the time comes for You to act, You will act. I may not always be faithful, but You always are. In a world where I am afraid to totally trust anyone, I know I can trust You. Thank You for being my Rock.

Day 36
The Lord Delivers

The Lord knoweth how to deliver
the godly out of temptations.
2 PETER 2:9

Self-control is not an easy path to follow. Those of us who try to follow You know it is steep, the footing insecure. Often it seems that others are standing at the edge of the path and throwing rocks under my feet, just to watch me stumble. If I lose my footing and fall, they take great pleasure in mocking me. Without Your help, I would fail to reach my goal; but You have promised that You will be there for me when I call for help. I do not know how to deliver myself from temptation, but You know the way. You have been there. You suffered temptation and won all Your trials. When I stumble, Your arms catch me; if I fall, You bring me to my feet and guide me onward.

Day 37
True Riches

That the generation to come might know them, even the children which should be born; who should arise and declare them to their children.

PSALM 78:6

I have an inheritance to pass on to my children, Lord—stories of Your power and deliverance, Your great works, and Your boundless love for all the generations before us and all those yet to come. I have little money or possessions for our children to inherit; but if I do my job well, they will be blessed with faith and empowered to pass that faith on to my grandchildren. What more could I possibly desire for them? Temporal riches are as nothing; they stay behind when we go to meet You. When times are hard and I become discouraged, be with me, Lord. Keep me a faithful teacher of the Way for the sake of my children and all those to come.

Day 38
Love

Know therefore that the LORD thy God,
he is God, the faithful God, which keepeth
covenant and mercy with them that love
him and keep his commandments to
a thousand generations.

DEUTERONOMY 7:9

Omnipotent Father, there are no limitations to the amount of love and attention You can bestow upon each of Your children. Although I receive Your rich blessings all the time, day and night, I pray that I will not take Your love for granted.

Lord, the more I know You and understand You, the more I will see and appreciate Your love. I pray that I will experience You more deeply so that my love for You will increase. You have taught me that sacrifices must be made for love to grow. I submit to You. Demolish me and then rebuild me so I may be one with You.

Day 39
Worry

*Which of you by taking thought
can add one cubit unto his stature?*
MATTHEW 6:27

Father, thanks for calming my agitation in times of distress. With Your peace, I smile at my foolish concerns: some situations are already past and cannot be changed; others were unlikely to happen; some were trivial and not worth my emotional energy—but worry turned a small concern into a long shadow. I could have changed only a few of the situations that troubled me.

Divine Father, equip me to deal with the problems over which I can make a difference. I pray that I will see my troubles more clearly with Your wisdom.

Day 40
Obedience in Doubt

But whoever has doubts is condemned if they eat, because their eating is not from faith; and everything that does not come from faith is sin.

ROMANS 14:23 NIV

The situation Paul talks of here is so strange to me, Lord. I've never had to think about eating meat sacrificed to idols. But I've doubted other Christians' actions and wondered if I should go along with them. Their faith seemed so strong compared to mine.

Thank You, Lord, for telling me not to listen to other people, but to You. Listening to others would confuse me, but You always give me the right advice. It doesn't matter what others think of me, as long as I'm walking down the path You have designed for me. Keep me walking with You and listening to Your still, small voice.

Day 41
God's Warning

*"Hear me, my people, and I will warn you—
if you would only listen to me, Israel!"*
PSALM 81:8 NIV

None of us can complain that You have not warned us, Lord. You've given us Your Word, let us run ourselves into trouble, and shown us that our own solutions go nowhere. Yet even though the message sounds loud and clear, we sometimes have a hard time heeding Your warning, Lord.

I want to pay attention to Your warnings, Lord, whether they come from Your Word, the results of a mistaken life choice, or another Christian. Help me discern what is of You, and open my ears wide for Your words.

Day 42
God's Messenger

*For the grace of God that bringeth
salvation hath appeared to all men,
teaching us that, denying ungodliness
and worldly lusts, we should live soberly,
righteously, and godly, in this present world.*

Titus 2:11–12

I try to be a good example of the Christian life,
Lord, so that those in the world can look at me
and perhaps begin to explore for themselves
the faith that guides my life. I witness in various
ways, depending on the gifts You have given
me, because I want everyone to experience Your
salvation.

I am not perfect. Others can always find fault
with me, no matter how I live, but I am only Your
messenger. Help me be a more effective witness
for You, I pray.

Day 43
Righteousness

The Lord openeth the eyes of the blind:
the Lord raiseth them that are bowed
down: the Lord loveth the righteous.
PSALM 146:8

Thank You, Lord God, for opening my eyes to see Your righteousness and raising me from my sin to new life in You. Without You, I would be blind and cast down by sin. But Your love changed my life from the ground up.

On my own, I am never righteous. Certainly You could never love me for my deeds. Yet in Your generous, gracious love, You cared for me even when I ignored You.

Help me to love others as You have loved me. I want to be part of Your mission to open blind eyes and raise cast-down hearts.

Day 44
When Things Go Wrong

For thou art my hope, O Lord GOD:
thou art my trust from my youth.
PSALM 71:5

Even as a child, Lord, I knew that things go wrong. Parents divorce, love is lost, pets die, and friends betray. As an adult, I know there are many things I cannot control, no matter how hard I may try; and many of life's events break my heart. But still I hope, because through it all I have You. You can heal even the deepest loss.

Thank You for this hope, for allowing me to lean on You in the bad times. With hope, anything is possible.

Day 45
The Offer

God setteth the solitary in families.
PSALM 68:6

Father, those who are happily married cannot understand how others can be happily single, just as parents cannot understand how others exist happily without children. You have provided for those who do not want a solitary existence, who need companionship and love to soften the daily rough spots of life, offering us marriage and parenthood. Not everyone will accept this offer, but that is their decision, and You respect their freedom of choice. I should do the same, no matter how strongly I feel they are missing some wonderful blessings. Constantly pushing others to find the right person (forgetting how difficult that can be) only discourages everyone. Give me the strength to let my children make their own decisions—no matter how much I personally want an armful of grandchildren to brighten my old age.

Day 46
Baby Food

*As newborn babes, desire the sincere milk
of the word, that ye may grow thereby.*
1 PETER 2:2

When I was a baby, I tried to eat anything I could hold in my hand, whether it was good for me or not. When I became a Christian, I did the same thing. I was in church several days a week. I read theology books I could not understand. I spent hours discussing faith with other students. It nearly made me sick. I was trying to eat the meat of faith with baby teeth. Fortunately, a kind pastor handed me a Bible and said, "Read this until you grow up a little. You're just a baby Christian now." I needed milk, not meat; and Your Bible nourished me completely. Even now, when I can digest everything better, Your Word is still the best food for me.

Day 47
Attitude

Create in me a clean heart, O God;
and renew a right spirit within me.
PSALM 51:10

Father, I am quick to focus on those things that affect me most directly. Often, I confess, I improperly view my wants as essentials. From minor matters such as restaurant service to more important ones such as making major purchases, I insist that my so-called requirements be fully met. I think and act as if those serving me should put my needs first.

Lord, keep a check on my attitude. I want to have a friendly disposition when I deal with others. Create in me a calm, controlled temperament. Help me have a "can do," "everything's okay" attitude rather than a "me" attitude.

Day 48
Panic

*And he said unto me, My grace is
sufficient for thee: for my strength
is made perfect in weakness.*
2 CORINTHIANS 12:9

Dear Lord, when evil unleashes its destructive
forces, I feel overwhelmed. Whether it is unexpected financial upheaval, a change in work as-
signment, an unfavorable doctor's report, or a
personal crisis, panic bubbles below the surface.
Dread hovers over me like an oppressive cloud
and dampens my spirit. Fear and doubt create
havoc in my otherwise rational mind.

Because panic becomes contagious and sets
off a frenzy around me, I must not give in to
panic. I pray for You to silence the alarms in my
life. Teach me to be composed in the midst of
uncertainty.

Day 49
More Like You

That they all may be one; as thou,
Father, art in me, and I in thee, that they
also may be one in us: that the world
may believe that thou hast sent me.

JOHN 17:21

Father, when I see an elderly couple that has spent a lifetime together in love, I find it remarkable how they anticipate one another's needs, how they communicate with merely a nod or a gesture, and, in some cases, how they have developed similar physical characteristics.

Father, I pray that during my life, I can in the same way become one with You. I want to absorb Your Word so thoroughly that I know Your will because it has become a part of me. I pray that I can talk with You easily and often because it has become my nature. And most of all, I pray that I will have the same spiritual characteristics as You.

Day 50
Aggressive Faith

I can do all things through Christ
which strengtheneth me.
PHILIPPIANS 4:13

Father, I go out each day as a soldier for You. If I am rewarded with victory after victory, may I examine my goals in case I am aiming too low. Teach me to see clearly the battles You want me to fight. Give me the ability to think the impossible, and fill me with the aggressive faith to make it happen.

Battles are long and victories are short. I would rather enjoy victories than failure, but I would rather suffer a lost battle than stand on the sidelines and do nothing. Almighty God, I surrender myself to Your service.

Day 51
Steadfast Faith

"Therefore I say to you, whatever things you ask when you pray, believe that you receive them, and you will have them."

MARK 11:24 NKJV

I'm so glad that all I have to do is believe, and I can receive the best from Your hand, Lord. But sometimes that believing is harder than it sounds. So many things—even good ones—can slide between my belief and the words I speak. Doubts often come to me more easily than faith.

On my own, I'm not very good at trusting You when life turns black. I tend to forget this verse or doubt that it's really for me. That's when I need to realize that my eyes are on the wrong thing—this world—when they should be on You.

Keep me steadfastly looking at You, Lord. Then I'll have all I could ask for.

Day 52
Protection from Evil

*But the Lord is faithful,
and he will strengthen you and
protect you from the evil one.*
2 Thessalonians 3:3 niv

When Satan attacks, Lord, I'm quickly aware of my own weakness. Though one minute I feel strong in You, in the next, the enemy's offensives suddenly threaten my faith. When evil pounds me, I thank You for offering me Your strength and protection. Without Your power, I'd be totally overwhelmed by the evil one.

Keep me from walking into Satan's traps, Lord. Protect me from unknowingly strolling down his ways. I don't want to get any closer to his dangers than I have to, and I won't if I'm walking close to Your side.

Today I need Your protection. You've promised to be there for me, and I need Your powerful defense now. Thank You, Lord.

Day 53
Sharing Jesus' Suffering

And since we are his children, we are his heirs. In fact, together with Christ we are heirs of God's glory. But if we are to share his glory, we must also share his suffering.
ROMANS 8:17 NLT

How many blessings You've given me, Lord. But just because I'm blessed with Your love doesn't mean I miss out on the hard times.

I have to admit I like the idea of sharing Your glory. That's the good part of this promise. I'm not so excited about sharing suffering. But help me to realize that these sufferings are shared. Whatever I have to go through, I don't do alone. Jesus, You've been there before me, and You walk by my side.

Thank You for sharing the hurts as well as the good things in life. I love You, Lord.

Day 54
The Sting of Reproach

*Blessed are ye, when men shall hate you,
and when they shall separate you from their
company, and shall reproach you, and cast out
your name as evil, for the Son of man's sake.*
LUKE 6:22

The sting of reproach frightens me, Lord, in whatever form it comes upon me. When I do Your work, I am vulnerable. Some will mock me and my beliefs; others will consider me dangerous—maybe even slightly crazy—or at least out of touch with modern life. Such experiences will tempt me to hold back when I know I should move forward boldly. Reproach hurts; I will do almost anything to avoid it.

Make me strong when I am weak; give me courage when I am afraid. If reproach comes to me, teach me how to deal with it in a godly manner for the sake of Your glory.

Day 55
A Prayer for Those in Need

Blessed is he that considereth the poor:
the Lord will deliver him in time of trouble.

PSALM 41:1

Father, today I pray for those who are struggling with poverty, those in my own community and throughout the world. Let me not fall into the trap of considering the poor as different from myself, for You know how rapidly fortunes can change and the wealthiest can fall into difficulty. Help me be generous with both my donations and my efforts to help those in need. The little I can contribute seems ineffective, but You will multiply it because I am Your child and precious in Your sight.

Day 56
"I Will Carry"

And even to your old age I am he;
and even to hoar hairs will I carry you:
I have made, and I will bear; even I
will carry, and will deliver you.

ISAIAH 46:4

Compassionate Father, Yours is the gift of long life; and I thank You for the bountiful years You have given me, years I never expected to see. Some people spend these extra years in good health until the end, but others bear the burden of poor health and failing finances.

I do not know which to expect, but I know I don't want my children to have to carry me during these years; they have their own burdens and need no more.

Thank You for Your help, support, and provision as I age. May I use these years to glorify Your love, so that my life will serve as an example to younger generations of Your strength and care.

Day 57
A Gift

If ye then, being evil, know how to give good gifts unto your children: how much more shall your heavenly Father give the Holy Spirit to them that ask him?

LUKE 11:13

Thank You, Father, for Your wonderful gift of the Holy Spirit. What better present could enable me to live in a fashion that pleases You? When Your Spirit fills me with power, I can live for You.

Without Your gift, I would be empty, Lord. Thank You for not only saving me through Your Son, Jesus, but giving me Your power to make each day count for You. I need Your gift every day. Help me not to leave Your Spirit on the shelf but to make Him part of my life always.

Day 58
Singing without Words

*Being filled with the fruits of
righteousness, which are by Jesus
Christ, unto the glory and praise of God.*
PHILIPPIANS 1:11

As a child, I never raised my hand in school unless it was obvious no one else wanted to answer. Then I would raise my hand to make my teacher feel better. The idea of speaking in public makes me physically ill. Even now, I could no more witness than I can fly. But You showed me other ways to witness and give praise and glory to God. When I help a neighbor in trouble, I am Your witness. When I tell a child about You, I am bearing good fruit. The same is true when I smile at a waitress or thank my doctor for his good care. Thank You for teaching me this, Lord. You have shown me how to sing without words and serve without notice.

Day 59
Belief

Believe ye that I am able to do this? They said
unto him, Yea, Lord. Then touched he their
eyes, saying, According to your faith be it
unto you. And their eyes were opened.
MATTHEW 9:28–30

I may pray day and night for healing, but without
believing in the One to whom I am praying, my
words are in vain. "According to your faith be it
unto you" is a great promise. It is also a condi-
tion for healing. Sometimes I forget this, Father.
I toss out prayer after prayer, just in case: in case
You are listening, in case nothing else works, in
case You can actually do this. On an ordinary day,
I do believe You are able to heal me, but sickness
frightens me, and I start qualifying every prayer.
Forgive my wavering, I pray. Strengthen my faith
and make me whole once more.

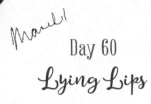

March 1

Day 60
Lying Lips

He that hideth hatred with lying lips,
and he that uttereth a slander, is a fool.
PROVERBS 10:18

Truthfulness is a great virtue to possess, but it's hard to maintain. Sometimes it seems easier and less cruel to go with a little lie, although it's never a wise move and will eventually cause more trouble than it's worth. But pretending to care for someone we dislike is nothing compared to slandering that person. Slander is a bald-faced lie about another. It's nearly always impossible for the victim to disprove the lie, so the social damage can be permanent.

Father, if I can't say anything nice about a person, at least keep me from slandering her. In the heat of anger, control my tongue, because what I say then can be as damaging to my soul as it is to my victim's reputation.

Day 61
Avoiding Sin

Be ye angry, and sin not: let not the
sun go down upon your wrath.
EPHESIANS 4:26

Father, You know all about anger because You have felt it Yourself. What You condemn is not anger itself but the sins anger gives rise to. It's what I do when I am angry that counts. Does my fury make me say words that hurt and will be remembered for years? Is my tone of voice a weapon instead of a healing salve? Do I belittle those I love in the heat of anger? Or do I remain as rational as possible, perhaps retreating until I can discuss the problem in a loving manner?

The next time I am angry, I pray You will guide me away from sin until I can speak words of peace and comfort once again. Help me be an example to my whole family.

Day 62
Jerusalem

And thy renown went forth among the heathen for thy beauty: for it was perfect through my comeliness, which I had put upon thee. . . . But thou didst trust in thine own beauty.
Ezekiel 16:14–15

Your chosen city, Jerusalem, was beautiful because of Your beauty, Father—a city made perfect through You. Its fame spread throughout the world; and, as people often do, its inhabitants began to take credit for the city's beauty themselves, believing that its beauty somehow came through their efforts and forgetting that its true foundation rested on You.

I tend to do the same today, taking credit for what I did not create on my own. Please don't let me fall into the trap of false pride. Whatever small beauty I bring into this world is only a tiny reflection of Your beauty, Your creation, Your perfection.

Day 63
Tongue Follows Heart

Before a word is on my tongue
you, LORD, know it completely.
PSALM 139:4 NIV

I can't keep a secret from You, Lord, because every word I speak is part of an open book. Before a syllable falls off my tongue, You know my thoughts and emotions. Words can't consistently hide feelings; eventually they'll directly reflect my heart and soul. In a sentence that shows what I really feel, truth finally comes out.

When I follow You closely, I need not worry. My words glorify You. Yet when I stray from You, my language changes, and people observe the alteration in my heart. Only if my heart is Yours will my words be too, Lord. May both constantly focus on You.

Day 64
Peace of Mind

*"I am leaving you with a gift—peace
of mind and heart. And the peace I
give is a gift the world cannot give.
So don't be troubled or afraid."*

JOHN 14:27 NLT

You know fear comes easily in this world, Lord. Maybe it's because You recognized how much we need Your special peace—surpassing anything this world has to offer—that You left Your people with this promise. Real peace is hard to come by here on earth.

When troubles come, help me to rest in You, Jesus, instead of accepting the world's turmoil. Truly, Your harmony isn't anything like this world's attempts at peacemaking—it reaches to my heart and soul and changes my life entirely. With it, the distress of the world remains at bay.

Thank You, Lord, for Your peace.

Day 65
The World's End

*I will punish the world for its evil,
the wicked for their sins. I will put an
end to the arrogance of the haughty and
will humble the pride of the ruthless.*
ISAIAH 13:11 NIV

Those who hate You don't win forever, Lord. I'm glad You've given us this promise so we know that whatever happens today isn't the end of the story. Though wicked people may seem to be on top now, either on this earth or in eternity, they will learn differently. The truths You've shown me in scripture will be proved right, and the wicked will not win.

But it doesn't have to end that way, if people recognize their sin today and turn from it. Use my witness to change lives on earth so some will have changed hearts—and changed eternities. Instead of settling for wickedness, let them live for You, Lord.

Day 66
God's Children

*For his Spirit joins with our spirit to
affirm that we are God's children.*
ROMANS 8:16 NLT

No matter what happens to my family, Lord,
Your Spirit has promised that I'm never alone.
I'm always part of Your family, which may have
members who get closer to my heart than
some of my blood relatives. If I lost everyone
You've given me—my parents, brothers, sisters, and my extended family—I'd still never be
alone. Thank You for caring so much for my
heart that You bring me family members who
love You, whether or not they're related by
blood.

I'm glad to be part of Your family. Help me
become a child You can be proud of, Lord.

Day 67
Trustworthiness

*"Whoever can be trusted with very
little can also be trusted with much,
and whoever is dishonest with very
little will also be dishonest with much."*
LUKE 16:10 NIV

If I'm trustworthy, You'll trust me with many things, Lord. But if I can't be trusted with earthly goods, You'll not offer me many heavenly benefits. How much I have isn't the issue—where my heart is makes the difference. I desire my soul to be set firmly on You.

I can also apply this verse to the people in my life. When others are trustworthy with small things, I'll be able to trust them with larger issues. Help me understand people's souls through their actions. Let me recognize those who don't know You, and pray for their hearts' redirection to faith.

Through Your Word and Spirit's guidance, help our human hearts become more trustworthy.

Day 68
Loving Unity

Can two walk together,
except they be agreed?
AMOS 3:3

Dear Lord, I am disheartened to encounter disagreement among those who profess to believe in You—fractured denominations, split congregations, and individuals who no longer speak to one another. We should be pulling together. Unfortunately, I confess that because of my own obstinance, I have contributed to the lack of harmony.

Lord, I pray that I will be more agreeable, that I will not be arrogant or unreasonable. Guide me to choose the right words that will lead to a better walk with You and with my brothers and sisters in Christ. Remind me that even if I am right, I can still be wrong if my comments are not wrapped in love.

Day 69
For Mercy

Be merciful unto me, O Lord:
for I cry unto thee daily.
PSALM 86:3

Father, sometimes You seem to be far from me. I look and see a great abyss between us; but as I pray, my vision clears and I perceive a bridge that was there all along. It is a bridge of mercy, constructed by You. Thank You for building the bridge that connects me to the peace You provide.

Sometimes I think I am not worthy of mercy and question how You can offer it to me. Implant in me the understanding that to appreciate Your mercy, I must show mercy to others. Banish from my heart the evil thought that others are not worthy of Your forgiving compassion.

Day 70
My Brothers and Sisters

He that loveth his brother abideth in the light, and there is none occasion of stumbling in him.
1 John 2:10

Lord Jesus, help me to love my brothers and sisters despite the distractions and troubles the world heaps on me. The things of this world will destroy my communion with You if I let them. Keep me mindful that discord with others also means I'm at war with You.

Instead of focusing on differences of opinions, help me look to You as an example of the perfect Brother. Then the small things will not make me stumble, and the large issues will be settled.

Day 71
God's Forgiveness

Let all bitterness, and wrath, and anger,
and clamour, and evil speaking, be put
away from you, with all malice: and be
ye kind one to another, tenderhearted,
forgiving one another, even as God for
Christ's sake hath forgiven you.
EPHESIANS 4:31–32

Father, You have taken my sins and put them far away from me, as if I had never sinned, for the sake of Jesus, my Redeemer. Yet still I fall victim to anger, wrath, and malice toward others, despite Your loving example. I live in a world full of anger, and I find forgiving difficult. In times of violent emotions, help me remember Your unending forgiveness and treat others with the kindness and compassion that You show to me every day of my life.

Day 72
The Salvation of All

*For this is good and acceptable in
the sight of God our Saviour; who will
have all men to be saved, and to come
unto the knowledge of the truth.*
1 TIMOTHY 2:3–4

Loving Father, only You know what is in a person's heart; only You are able to judge and save. You say it is Your desire that all should be saved and know Your truth, that through Your Son You have made salvation available to me if I but ask for it. I thank You for this greatest blessing of all.

Remind me that I am not Your gatekeeper or Your judge. My task is to spread the joyful Gospel to all, to believe You will make my efforts fruitful, and never to stand in the way of another's salvation. Open my heart, show me where I am needed, and I will trust the rest to You.

Day 73
Seeking God

The LORD is with you, while ye be with him;
and if ye seek him, he will be found of you;
but if ye forsake him, he will forsake you.
2 CHRONICLES 15:2

Lord, You showed me Your wonderful salvation, using Your people to draw me to Your love. When I knew nothing of You, You prepared a way for me to accept You.

How can I repay Your gift of freedom from sin? I own nothing valuable enough to repay the life of Your Son. Even if I give You each and every day of the rest of my life, the gift would be too small.

But take my life. Keep me strong in You; forsaking You would be too painful a thing to imagine. My life is Yours, Father. May I honor You all my days.

Day 74
Dignity

Honour thy father and thy mother.
EXODUS 20:12

In time, I may have to begin to play a more active role in the lives of my aging parents, Lord. My mother may need help with the shopping; my father may need to be convinced he should not drive anymore. I may have to help balance their checkbook or help with their investments. This can be a difficult time for all of us, especially if they feel they are a burden. I ask Your help when this time comes. Remind me that their dignity must be preserved whenever I need to help them. Keep me tactful, allowing them as much self-control as possible within the bounds of safety and honoring their wishes above my own. They gave me so much; now it is my honor to give to them.

Day 75
Giving with Joy

Every man according as he purposeth in his heart, so let him give; not grudgingly, or of necessity: for God loveth a cheerful giver.
2 Corinthians 9:7

Lord, sometimes I start out to give generously but end up putting the large bill back in my wallet and finding a smaller one to put in the plate. Other times I see my pew-mates giving more than I have out, so I quickly exchange the bills again because I feel pressured to be more generous. By the time the plate is out of sight, I don't feel at all cheerful. I know that no one really cares what I give. I am putting the pressure on myself and can blame no one but myself. Don't let me feel social pressure that's not even there, Father. No matter how much or how little I can donate, I should give joyously.

Day 76
The Lesson

Now no chastening for the present seemeth to be joyous, but grievous: nevertheless afterward it yieldeth the peaceable fruit of righteousness unto them which are exercised thereby.

HEBREWS 12:11

Oh Lord, I'm certain that You occasionally have to go to great lengths to get my attention. Yet because I know you as a loving Father, I rarely think that my troubles may indeed be coming as Your means of correcting me. But sometimes when problems pile up, I have to stop and think, *Did I do something that needs correcting?* I take time to confess my faults and ask Your forgiveness, secure that You will forgive even my hidden sins. Even if my prayer does not solve all my problems, it does bring me back to You; and perhaps that was the lesson I needed to learn in the first place.

Day 77
Worldly Correction

For our light affliction, which is but for a moment, worketh for us a far more exceeding and eternal weight of glory.
2 Corinthians 4:17

The world "corrects" me every day, Father, quite often unjustly and in no way to my benefit. At the time, the blows I suffer seem to be more than I can bear. But with Your help I do bear them; and when I bear them through faith, my actions are examples of Your power and love. The worst the world can do is kill me. I'm not exactly eager for that, Father, but when the time comes, I pray I will be able to bear death as well as I bore life, secure in Your love and looking to the salvation You have promised is mine. Until then I will do my best to be Your witness here on earth.

Day 78
Exile

*For the eyes of the Lord are over the
righteous, and his ears are open unto
their prayers: but the face of the Lord
is against them that do evil.*
1 PETER 3:12

I cannot imagine what it would feel like to know
that You have turned Your face away from me,
Lord. You would look after the righteous but
never even see me. You would answer their
prayers but choose not to even hear mine. I
would not exist to You. What loneliness! What
fear and desolation. Of course I am thankful for
the love and care You show to me, but I take no
pleasure from the suffering of those You have
turned away from. If it is in Your will, rid them
of their evil ways so they can be touched by Your
love again, made whole, and brought back into
fellowship with those who follow You.

Day 79
The Genuine Article

Whatsoever things are true, whatsoever things are honest, whatsoever things are just, whatsoever things are pure, whatsoever things are lovely, whatsoever things are of good report. . .think on these things.

PHILIPPIANS 4:8

Father, I can see in my daily activities how people strive for easy perfection—a mathematical "proof" that solves a problem in the least number of steps, a musical composition without a discordant note, a work of art that achieves harmony and symmetric composition.

Dear Lord, I strive for a life in tune with Your orchestration.

I know that to have an honorable life, I must be meticulous in eliminating the inferior elements and strive to reflect Your higher nature. I want to be a genuine Christian. I put my life in Your hands so that I can come closer to reaching that goal.

Day 80
Enter with Thanksgiving

And God said unto Moses, I AM THAT I AM:
and he said, Thus shalt thou say unto the
children of Israel, I AM hath sent me unto you.
EXODUS 3:14

Father, I pray that I may always enter Your presence in the proper way. I resolve to acknowledge with thanksgiving what You have done for me. You are merciful, long-suffering, and mindful of me. I praise You for the blessings that flow from You.

Lord, I come before You with humility. I bow before You, the Creator who called everything into existence. I bow in awe of You as I realize You are the I AM, the eternal presence that has spanned the ages. I humbly cry to You as my provider and deliverer.

Day 81
Synchronize

And God said, Let there be lights in the firmament of the heaven to divide the day from the night; and let them be for signs, and for seasons, and for days, and years.

GENESIS 1:14

I've stopped wearing a watch, Lord, not because time is no longer important to me, but because everywhere I go, clocks, watches, and electronic gadgets constantly show the time. My microwave, car radio, and computer screen display the time. The time is everywhere!

Lord, You created time and gave us the dependable progression of the sun, moon, and stars to mark off days, seasons, and years. Help me recognize each moment as a gift from You. I pray that I will plan my day to be in sync with Your eternal purposes.

Day 82
End of Sin

*Therefore, since Christ suffered for us
in the flesh, arm yourselves also with
the same mind, for he who has suffered
in the flesh has ceased from sin.*
1 PETER 4:1 NKJV

Though I don't relish the tough times, Lord, I have to admit I'd like to be done with sin. No matter how much I try to avoid it, sin influences me constantly—and if I'm not careful, I easily find myself slipping into it again.

I'm glad my suffering has a purpose in Your plan, though I may not completely understand the details. How wonderful to know that suffering, however painful, will make me pure because of Your Son's sacrifice.

I want to cease from sin, Lord. Make me pure in You.

Day 83
Blessings of Work

*For the LORD your God will bless you in all
your harvest and in all the work of your
hands, and your joy will be complete.*
DEUTERONOMY 16:15 NIV

I'll admit I don't always recognize the blessings
of work, Lord. When things are too challenging,
it's hard to imagine any job is a blessing. When I
have to find a new, permanent job that will help
me plan my future, "blessing" may not be the
first word that comes to mind.

But like the people who celebrated their
harvest, I like knowing that my life is provided
for. Having a regular paycheck shows You are
caring for my life. So put me in the place where
You'd have me work. As I labor for You, Lord,
You bless me, and I discover the complete joy of
relying on You.

Day 84
The Value of Knowledge

Gold there is, and rubies in abundance,
but lips that speak knowledge are a rare jewel.
PROVERBS 20:15 NIV

Lord, You know gold and jewels have their attraction for me. The things of this world look good to me, or they'd never be a temptation. Satan's aware of that and uses things to his advantage. But You've warned me that the real jewels of heaven do not sparkle physically. Knowledge of You and Your Word are the truly valuable things—on earth and in heaven.

I may never own the jewels and metals many people treasure here, but I'm glad I know You and can send this jewel into eternity. Earning Your "well done" means more to me than any earthly thing.

Day 85
Greatness in Service

*"The greatest among you
will be your servant."*
MATTHEW 23:11 NIV

It's hard to think of greatness in servanthood, Lord. Our world doesn't think that way, and breaking out of the mold takes effort. Even in church I can have a hard time seeing greatness as a matter of doing things for others.

Help me change my thinking, Jesus, and help me model the lifestyle You want every Christian to have. Instead of seeking personal fame or self-importance, I need to help others and aid them in drawing closer to You. When other people see my actions, I want them to see You.

Help me become Your servant in every way, Lord. Then I'll have the only greatness worth having—I will be distinguished in Your eyes.

Day 86
The Gift of Salvation

*Not by works of righteousness which we
have done, but according to his mercy he
saved us, by the washing of regeneration,
and renewing of the Holy Ghost.*
TITUS 3:5

Salvation cannot be earned; grace cannot be demanded as payment for my services. No matter how I strive to live in righteousness, I will always fall short of Your standards. You know this, gracious Father; otherwise You would not have sent Your Son for the salvation of all who claim His name.

But You did send Him, and the Holy Ghost is with me today because of my neediness. Thank You for making my perfection possible in the life to come. By myself, I would certainly fail. With You, anything is possible.

Day 87
"Don't Be Afraid"

Fear not, little flock; for it is your Father's
good pleasure to give you the kingdom.
LUKE 12:32

Don't be afraid. How many times have I said that to my children? I know that nightmares are not real and not every barking dog bites. I know that eating spinach is not fatal and that even the darkest night is followed by a bright sunrise. Yet still they have fears I cannot ease.

I come to You like the child I am, Father, still afraid of the dark that lingers in my mind. You take great pleasure in me, anxious to give me Your kingdom, but my fears hold me back. Help me to trust in Your love the way my children trust in mine, for only then will I experience the joyful life You have designed me to live.

Day 88
Slack Hands

He becometh poor that dealeth
with a slack hand: but the hand
of the diligent maketh rich.
PROVERBS 10:4

It's so easy to fall prey to the "slack-hand syndrome," Lord. Sometimes I can do my work without ever engaging my brain. A job that was once a challenge is soon mastered, and I find myself growing bored and sloppy, cutting corners, giving less and less of myself. .

Help me see these symptoms when they first appear and do something to change my work habits. Perhaps I need more responsibilities and challenges; perhaps a minor reality check is in order. I want to be known as a diligent worker, not someone with slack hands. Thank You for Your guidance, Lord.

Day 89
Spiritual Poverty

Blessed are the poor in spirit:
for theirs is the kingdom of heaven.
MATTHEW 5:3

Being poor in spirit doesn't seem like an attractive thing, Lord. It's not something I'd think to covet. But if I'd never realized how needy I was, I'd never have come to You with my sins. Thank You for showing me my poverty and promising me Your kingdom in return for my sin.

As I grow in faith, I'm often tempted to ignore my poverty and become proud in the changes You've brought into my life. I start to take credit for things You've done. Remind me then of my need for You, the source of my spiritual riches. Without You, I am poor, yet You offer me the riches of heaven. I am blessed indeed.

Day 90
Taking Matters into My Own Hands

A faithful man shall abound with blessings: but he that maketh haste to be rich shall not be innocent.

PROVERBS 28:20

Father, You give richly to Your children. Everything I need to live a fulfilling life is mine for the asking, but blessings come in Your time, not mine. Sometimes I grow weary of waiting, thinking that if I could only have a little more money, I would be even happier. I give up on faithful waiting and take matters into my own hands. I work long hours, ignoring the needs of my family. I harden my heart and walk over others at work to get to the next level. I hide my wallet when those in need ask me for help.

Help me keep my priorities in order, Father, trusting that You will provide what I need, when I need it, and how I need it.

Day 91
In God's Season

I am the vine, ye are the branches:
he that abideth in me, and I in him,
the same bringeth forth much fruit:
for without me ye can do nothing.
JOHN 15:5

Father, sometimes I get ahead of You, so determined to bear fruit that it never dawns on me that fruit has its own season, and apple trees don't bear in March. Sometimes I'm just innocently eager; other times my pride is running the show. Either way, those apples will develop when You want them to, not when I say so; and I need to keep that in mind as I set out to accomplish Your work.

When some worthwhile project of mine fails for no obvious reason, remind me that I may be working out of season. I need to get in step with Your timetable.

Day 92
Cleansing Prayer

And when ye stand praying, forgive,
if ye have ought against any: that your
Father also which is in heaven may
forgive you your trespasses.
MARK 11:25

Lord, You make it quite clear that forgiveness is a vital preparation for worship. In fact, it should come before my other prayers, since the forgiveness of my sins depends on my forgiveness of others. If I go to services without forgiving, I set up a roadblock between myself and You, which is the last thing I want, since only You can forgive me. Forgiving those who have wronged me is not something I enjoy doing, but it is simply good hygiene, like washing my hands before eating. Remind me of this every time I go to worship, Lord. Give me the strength to forgive others so You will forgive me my own trespasses.

Day 93
Finding the Shoreline

Thy word is a lamp unto my feet,
and a light unto my path.
PSALM 119:105

If there's one thing I need, it's trustworthy guidance, Lord. There is plenty of advice available to me in these modern times. The internet is full of it—some good, some bad. If I prefer hard copy, thousands of books are published every year on religion and ethics. Even television offers all types of advice for all types of problems, if I take it to heart or not. If I took all the advice I hear seriously, I would be driven like a wave from one place to another without ever finding the shoreline. There is only one way to reach the path to the beach: trusting in Your Word. In darkness or light, on fair days or foul, I can trust the light of Your Word to bring me safely home.

Day 94
Planning

A man's heart deviseth his way:
but the LORD directeth his steps.
PROVERBS 16:9

I have made lots of plans in my lifetime, Father, some of them just wishful thinking, some very concrete and detailed. They were all good for mental discipline, but not all that many worked out the way I thought they would. Some I was not at all suited for; others would take me two lifetimes to complete. Still, it's good to have some idea of where I want to go and what I will need along the way. Not all my plans are in Your will, though—even those that sound like good ideas to me. When they are not, You show me a better idea, and I thank You for Your guidance. Keep me on the right path when my own plans are flawed, because only You know where You need me to be today and tomorrow.

Day 95
Joy in the Journey

*Thou preparest a table before me in the
presence of mine enemies: thou anointest
my head with oil; my cup runneth over.*
PSALM 23:5

Dear Lord, when I was a child, my father drove
me along a road toward where a rainbow seemed
to end just over the next hill. But no matter how
far we traveled, we never reached the end of
the rainbow. It was always ahead of us. Later,
as an adult, I discovered that no matter what I
achieved, contentment stayed out of reach.

Father, thank You for showing me that contentment is not a destination but a journey.
Rather than becoming discontented and looking
for a better situation, I pray I will focus on what
You have given me. May I see my cup as running
over with Your blessings.

Day 96
Honor

*And he said unto him, Behold now,
there is in this city a man of God,
and he is an honourable man; all that
he saith cometh surely to pass: now
let us go thither; peradventure he can
shew us our way that we should go.*
1 Samuel 9:6

Thank You, Lord, for the place of honor You give me in Your Kingdom. As armor helps keep a warrior safe in battle, You shield me from the fiery darts of evil. It is Your assistance that makes it possible for me to live an honorable life. I need Your protective covering to cast off the works of darkness.

Lord, help me live a consistent life so that those who don't know You will be drawn to You. I pray that I will have a good name in the community and that I will direct others to heaven.

Day 97
Illuminate but Don't Blind

*Ye are all the children of light,
and the children of the day: we are
not of the night, nor of darkness.*
1 THESSALONIANS 5:5

Lord, the other night during a power failure, I was the first to find a flashlight. The little light was enough to dispel the darkness. Because I carried the light, my family members gathered around me.

Your radiance illuminates all creation, yet I see people stumbling in spiritual gloom. Although I am but a pale reflection of Your brilliance, I pray that my teaching will become a beacon that draws lost souls into the circle of Your light. May my light never dazzle but rather reveal. Guide me so that I push out the darkness and fill others' lives with the light of Christ.

Day 98
Overcoming the World

*Who is he that overcometh the
world, but he that believeth
that Jesus is the Son of God?*
1 John 5:5

When worldly temptations press in on me, I'm glad You gave me this promise, Jesus. It's hard to be in the world and not fall into its traps. But as I believe in You, who have overcome the world, I overcome it too. I don't have to settle for giving in to the world's temptations and wickedness. You've given me the ability to fight back in You—and to win through You.

I want to enjoy Your blessings for this life without being trapped in wrong thoughts or actions. Where You have overcome, I don't need to be defeated. Keep me faithful to You, Jesus, and my battle will be won.

Day 99
Valued by God

*"And the very hairs on your head
are all numbered. So don't be afraid;
you are more valuable to God than
a whole flock of sparrows."*
LUKE 12:7 NLT

Sparrows aren't very important, Lord, yet You take care of even these small birds. Though some people may think them a nuisance, You know when each one falls.

Maybe it's not a huge compliment to be compared to sparrows, but I get Your message loud and clear. Everything about me, even down to how many hairs are on my head, is important to You. If You care about the birds, how much more important am I to You.

Thank You for having compassion even about the tiny things in my life. With that kind of concern, You're teaching me that I don't have to worry about a thing.

Day 100
God's Protection

*He will cover you with his feathers,
and under his wings you will find refuge;
his faithfulness will be your shield and
rampart. You will not fear the terror of
night, nor the arrow that flies by day.*
PSALM 91:4–5 NIV

When You are protecting me, Lord, there's nothing I need to fear. Still, I have a hard time grasping such a weighty promise. Though my mind accepts it, it's so easy to believe otherwise when I face dangers in life. Before I even think about it, I find myself trusting in the things of this world for my protection. I look to friends, family, or government for safety instead of looking to You.

Remind me, when I face troubles, that I need only turn to You. Then, day or night, I'm perfectly safe.

Day 101
Teaching about Jesus

These are the things that ye shall do;
Speak ye every man the truth to his
neighbour; execute the judgment of
truth and peace in your gates.
ZECHARIAH 8:16

Lord Jesus, I occasionally take on the role of teacher, although I often feel inadequate for the task. My goal is to be a mentor, guide, and advisor. May I grow in knowledge, wisdom, character, and confidence so I can help those I teach to choose the proper path.

Heavenly Teacher, provide me with the ability to instill in my students a love for learning more about You, reading the Bible, talking to You in prayer, and living a life in keeping with Your Word. May I have an influence that will last a lifetime.

Day 102
Lacking Nothing

Fear the LORD, you his holy people,
for those who fear him lack nothing.
PSALM 34:9 NIV

Lacking nothing: what a wonderful feeling that would be. I admit I often don't feel You've entirely fulfilled this promise in my life. Then I'm reminded of all the things You provide for me because I fear You: spiritual peace; enough money to cover my real needs, even if I don't get everything I want; people who love me; and a thousand other things I tend to take for granted.

Help me not to look at things I'd like to have and feel as if I'm missing out. They are really "extras" I can live comfortably without. You do provide me with all the things I really need.

As long as I fear You, Lord, I never need to fear the future.

Day 103
Hold My Hand

*I am continually with thee: thou
hast holden me by my right hand.
Thou shalt guide me with thy counsel,
and afterward receive me to glory.*
PSALM 73:23–24

Often I am like a little child in a big toy store,
running from aisle to aisle and asking for everything that looks good. Sometimes You grant me
my wish; other times You say no. Like a loving
parent, You hold me by the hand so I don't get
lost in the store, just as my mother always did.
Like my mother, You point out when my wishes
are poorly made or too expensive for my soul. I
admit that once in a while I have a temper tan-
trum, disputing Your guidance and wanting my
own way, but You have never been wrong. Thank
You for Your love and patience, for I will always
need Your guidance.

Day 104
The Golden Rule

Therefore all things whatsoever ye would that men should do to you, do ye even so to them: for this is the law and the prophets.
MATTHEW 7:12

Lord, I have memorized the Bible verse that is called the Golden Rule. Yet, putting it into practice is far more difficult than learning the words. While You were here on earth, You demonstrated the perfect example of living out this principle.

Jesus, I praise You for showing me compassion and granting me forgiveness for my transgressions. Thank You for teaching me how to have peace in my life. Lord, give me the determination to do unto others as I want them to do unto me.

Day 105
A Resolute Heart

But Daniel purposed in his heart that he would not defile himself with the portion of the king's meat, nor with the wine which he drank: therefore he requested of the prince of the eunuchs that he might not defile himself.

DANIEL 1:8

Heavenly Father, despite the quiet time I am experiencing now, I know that challenges will test me—if not later today, then sometime soon. Once temptations are upon me, there is seldom adequate time or the proper environment to make a reasoned response. My goal is to look ahead, consider the evils I may face, and make the right decision before the events occur.

Even so, Lord, after I make an important decision, there is a time of second-guessing, both from myself and from others. Rid my mind of doubts that serve no useful end. I pray I will be resolute and boldly live a consistent, purposeful life.

Day 106
A Divine Master

But without faith it is impossible to please him: for he that cometh to God must believe that he is, and that he is a rewarder of them that diligently seek him.

HEBREWS 11:6

Lord, I know of a bronze statue in Edinburgh, Scotland, that commemorates a Skye terrier named Greyfriars Bobby. After his owner died, this dog followed the funeral procession to the churchyard where they buried his master. The terrier stayed near the grave for the next fourteen years.

Divine Master, when You died, You died because of my sins. I want to dedicate my life to You. I will show my loyalty by being faithful to Your Church and devoted to my family. My eyes will remain fixed on Calvary. Your cross demonstrates the truth that You will never leave me or forsake me.

Day 107
Brotherly Love

*But as touching brotherly love ye need not that
I write unto you: for ye yourselves are taught of
God to love one another.*

1 Thessalonians 4:9

Lord, You have brought us together, sons and
daughters all, and made us into one family,
teaching every one of us to love our brothers and sisters in Christ. We are Your Church.
We are different in many ways: rich and poor,
black and white, male and female. Some of us
lead and some follow, each according to the
talents You have given us and the needs of the
community. In many ways we are more different than we are alike, yet Your love for us knows
no human boundaries. We are family. We are
Your Church.

Day 108
Giving in Faith

But when thou makest a feast, call the poor, the maimed, the lame, the blind: and thou shalt be blessed; for they cannot recompense thee: for thou shalt be recompensed at the resurrection of the just.
LUKE 14:13–14

Father, sometimes charity seems to be a thankless task. No one will ever repay me, and I see no immediate results to give me some sense of satisfaction. It's like dropping a penny into a bottomless well: I can't even hear it clink at the end of its fall.

Remind me that though the little I can give seems useless, when added to the little that millions give, my charity can make a difference. You recall every penny I drop into the alms box; the consequences of my charity are in Your hands. Help me to give in faith.

Day 109
New Life

*Therefore if any man be in Christ, he is
a new creature: old things are passed
away; behold, all things are become new.*
2 Corinthians 5:17

Sometimes I feel so clean, Lord, when I've confessed sin and put it far behind me. Then I know the truth of this verse. Other times, even when I'm serving You, I feel dull and slightly used.

Thank You that Your salvation reaches beyond my feelings. It doesn't matter how I feel. When sin causes me to feel doubt or dullness, You don't toss me out of Your kingdom, but call me to new faith. I need You to renew me constantly.

Make me new again this day.

Day 110
A Prayer of Faith

And the prayer of faith shall save the sick,
and the Lord shall raise him up; and if he have
committed sins, they shall be forgiven him.
JAMES 5:15

Father, today I pray for the sick among us, those whom medicine has failed, those whose only hope remains in Your compassion and power. You may or may not choose to heal those I lift up to You, but I know You have the power, if earthly healing is in Your will.

I ask You to cleanse their souls as well as their bodies, to keep them strong in the faith no matter what befalls them, and to be a source of comfort to those who love them. Stand by them all in their time of suffering, wrap them in Your arms of love, and if You choose, heal their earthly bodies.

Day 111
The Pathway

*And thine ears shall hear a word behind
thee, saying, This is the way, walk ye
in it, when ye turn to the right hand,
and when ye turn to the left.*

ISAIAH 30:21

If life is like a pathway in the woods, I'm always making problems for myself along the way. The woods are deep and dark, and I am easily distracted. I go off to the left to find a hidden spring that I can hear bubbling up, only to lose the path. I follow the tracks of a deer until sunset and barely find shelter before darkness falls. I make the same mistakes on the path of life, losing sight of the trail and calling out for You to find me before it's too late and I am lost forever.

Thank You for finding me, Lord, for putting my feet back on the path and leading me home.

Day 112
Quietness of Spirit

Better is an handful with quietness,
than both the hands full with
travail and vexation of spirit.
ECCLESIASTES 4:6

I confess that I am easily vexed, Lord, but it is just the grouchiness of old age, not true vexation of my spirit. I have been blessed with a good life. I learned to live the simple life as a child, when we didn't have much money but always had fun. I learned to be thankful when my children were born. I learned to give when others gave to me. I have also discovered that the world is full of very nice people doing their best under the circumstances. Oh, there are a few stinkers in the crowd, but overall I like people. Thank You for all You have given me, Lord, for all You have taught me, and for all the good times still to come.

Day 113
An Instant World

For ye have need of patience, that,
after ye have done the will of God,
ye might receive the promise.
Hebrews 10:36

This is an instant world, Lord. Patience is not much valued here. If I don't get what I think I need, I take charge myself and double my efforts, not even thinking about sitting back in patience and waiting for You to act. Like a little child, I run to and fro looking for something to amuse me, even when I know it's not amusement I need. Just like a child, I get myself in trouble when I run ahead of You. On days when I go off on my own, draw me close to You until I calm down and begin to think clearly. Everything is under control. All I need has been provided. All I need to contribute is faith and patience.

Day 114
Worry

Therefore take no thought, saying,
What shall we eat? or, What shall we drink?
or, Wherewithal shall we be clothed?...
For your heavenly Father knoweth that
ye have need of all these things.
MATTHEW 6:31–32

Worry is our most useless emotion. It is unproductive and dangerous. Sometimes it may prod me into taking action to save myself, but even then there is no guarantee that my actions will be effective, because I do not think rationally when I am consumed with worry. Most of the time, worry disables me, locks me in my room, separates me from those who would be willing to help. It convinces me that I am unworthy, or stupid, or unforgiven—all lies of the devil, not Your judgments. Being concerned about my future is one thing; letting worry cripple me is a lack of faith. You know what I need, Lord, and You will provide.

Day 115
Life Purity

*Wives, in the same way submit yourselves
to your own husbands so that, if any of
them do not believe the word, they may be won
over without words by the behavior
of their wives, when they see the purity
and reverence of your lives.*
1 PETER 3:1–2 NIV

Just imagine—I can live so well in purity that I win someone to You, Lord! What a blessing to know that a spotless life that depicts Your love can bring those I love to faith, even if I don't say a word.

Thank You, Jesus, for making my life that valuable. Help me to live so well that I become a beacon to my family and friends. Every day I want to shine forth Your love and grace.

Day 116
Wisdom against Strife

Mockers stir up a city,
but the wise turn away anger.
PROVERBS 29:8 NIV

Plenty of people can tear down, but building up a leader so that problems can be solved is a better solution, Lord. I recognize that. Yet I've found it easy enough to criticize or condemn a boss, a politician, or a church leader.

Instead of rushing to attack a person or a situation, I want to become a problem solver—one who turns to You for the right, peaceful solution. So move my heart far from anger and hurt, and give me Your peace to share with others. Help me not to mock them, but to turn aside anger and find a real solution. Then I know I'll be doing Your will.

Day 117
Evil and Fear

Everyone who does evil hates the light,
and will not come into the light for fear
that their deeds will be exposed.
JOHN 3:20 NIV

Lord, I'm glad I don't have to worry about this negative promise. Because I've trusted completely in You, I never have to fear Your light. My life can be open to You because You have cleansed my heart.

But those who are evil do fear Your light. They may try to envelop their sin in a haze of lies and prevarication, but they can't hide from You. Make me aware of those who love Your light and those who turn from it. I want to share Your light with those who need it and rejoice in the light with my brothers and sisters. Thank You, Lord, for Your light.

Day 118
The Power of the Word

For our gospel came not unto you in word only, but also in power, and in the Holy Ghost, and in much assurance; as ye know what manner of men we were among you for your sake.
1 THESSALONIANS 1:5

Lord, I confess to You that I often read the Bible hurriedly and without much comprehension. Despite my sometimes superficial reading, I do gain something from staying in touch with You. More gratifying, though, are those occasions when I take the time to think upon Your Word and meditate upon Your message. Most useful of all are those occasions when certain passages capture my attention. For several days I carry the verses around in my thoughts and pray about them. Slowly, by continually holding them in my mind, they dawn into full light.

Father, I pray that the power of Your Word will transform my mind. Change the printed words into words written on my heart and living in my spirit.

Day 119
Rooted in Jesus

*As ye have therefore received Christ
Jesus the Lord, so walk ye in him: rooted
and built up in him, and stablished in the
faith, as ye have been taught, abounding
therein with thanksgiving.*

COLOSSIANS 2:6–7

As I hiked along a wilderness trail today, Lord, I stepped over some tree roots projecting above the ground. I was reminded of the importance of good root systems. I could not see most of the roots, but I could see the tall trees they supported. Without a strong root system, the trees could not stand upright. The trunk and branches above the ground could not survive without the water and nutrients provided by the roots.

Lord, Your creation provides me with visual applications to my spiritual life. I need to be rooted in Your Word to be a strong, stable Christian. You, Lord Jesus, are the water and food that I seek to support my spiritual life and health.

Day 120
Uprightness

*He kneeled upon his knees three times
a day, and prayed, and gave thanks
before his God, as he did aforetime.*
DANIEL 6:10

Lord, I want to live an upright life no matter how difficult the circumstances. I look to Daniel as an example of one who was not afraid to do what was right, even though he faced death in a den of lions. You gave him protection and blessed his integrity.

When I face tough times, I pray I will continue to put my trust in You, Lord. Give me a strong faith like Daniel's. You are more powerful than the enemy of my soul, and You have every situation in my life under control.

Day 121
Healed by Jesus

But he was wounded for our transgressions,
he was bruised for our iniquities: the
chastisement of our peace was upon him;
and with his stripes we are healed.
ISAIAH 53:5

Lord, I do not know how often You have restored my health. I may have never seen or understood many of Your actions, and I may often credit others for what was actually Your healing and preservation. But I know You are always with me, and I thank You for Your protection.

Father God, You have promised I have healing in Jesus. No illness is beyond Your power, Lord. When I suffer from sin or physical pain, keep me mindful that Your hand is still on me. May each trial strengthen me spiritually and draw me nearer to You. Ultimately, I will experience Your healing—here or in heaven.

Keep me mindful of the price Your Son paid so I could enjoy a healthy relationship with You. Let my trust in You never fail.

Day 122
The Company of Sinners

For I am not come to call the righteous,
but sinners to repentance.
MATTHEW 9:13

Father, examine the way I use my time in Your service. Am I too comfortable? Do I spend my time in fellowship with other believers because it is pleasant and safe, or do I risk the company of sinners? Who needs me most, my neighbor in the pew or my brother and sister in need of repentance and forgiveness? How can I be more effective in my outreach and missionary work?

Your Son showed me by example how I should be spending my time. Give me the strength and courage to make the hard choices, to go where I am needed, to minister to those seemingly beyond help—to risk the company of sinners.

Day 123
God's Power

But thus saith the LORD, Even the captives
of the mighty shall be taken away, and the prey
of the terrible shall be delivered: for I
will contend with him that contendeth with thee,
and I will save thy children.

ISAIAH 49:25

No matter what power attacks me, Lord, and seeks to imprison me, it holds no sway over me. When I am right with You, no authority, not even Satan, can place me beyond Your deliverance.

Thank You, Lord, for being my protector, no matter what situation I find myself in. Whether I become a political prisoner or am tied hand and foot by sin, I can trust in Your deliverance as I continue in Your love.

Deliver me, Lord, from all that binds me. I cannot free myself.

Day 124
Not Forsaken

But I am poor and needy;
yet the Lord thinketh upon me.
PSALM 40:17

Who am I to come to You with prayers and thanksgiving, Lord? Who cares what I think? I am not a great person—not even a particularly good person. I will never do wonderful things or be loved by everyone who knows me. I will spend my life in loneliness and fear, just another nobody in a world full of nobodies.

But still You think about me. You don't just notice me and pass on—You actually take the time to think about me, to pay attention to me, to help me when I need help, and to protect me when I need protecting. I am not alone; I am not forsaken. Thank You, Lord!

Day 125
Keeping the Temple

Know ye not that your body is the temple
of the Holy Ghost which is in you, which ye have
of God, and ye are not your own?
1 Corinthians 6:19

Self-control is not a widespread virtue today, Lord. Many pervert the concept, turning it into "It's my body, and I can do what I want," when its true meaning is more like "It's God's body, and I need to control myself." My body is Your temple, the home of the Holy Spirit that lives in me and guides me. Why would I ever want to defile this temple for some fleeting pleasure? Of course I am tempted—I am fully human—but this body was made by You to glorify You, not myself. Be with me when I am tempted, Lord. Show me the true joys of self-control, I pray.

Day 126
Wasting Time

Favour is deceitful, and beauty is vain:
but a woman that feareth the LORD,
she shall be praised.
PROVERBS 31:30

I know friends come and go, whether they are rich and powerful or just ordinary people. Currying favor with the "right people" is rarely worth the trouble. They have nothing I want and will soon move on to other friends because I have nothing they want. Seeking personal beauty is likewise a waste of time. I may be able to hide the toll of time for a little while, but eventually the wrinkles will prevail. Help me invest my precious time in more worthy pursuits, Lord, ones that will provide lasting satisfaction. I'm not sure what You will ask of me, but I am willing to try anything You recommend and give any resulting praise to You, where it belongs.

Day 127
Looking in All the Wrong Places

If any of you lack wisdom, let him ask of God, that giveth to all men liberally, and upbraideth not; and it shall be given him.

JAMES 1:5

Embracing wisdom is not difficult for a child of God; finding it is harder. In our search for wisdom, we often chase after it in the wrong places. The evening news may give us the facts, but its interpretation of the facts is often flawed. Professors try to build wisdom through the teachings of knowledge, but a wise student carefully evaluates any conclusions a teacher draws from the facts.

Only You are the perfect source of wisdom, Father. You give it to us liberally when we ask for it, never considering us stupid or leading us astray. You have given us Your Word as the best schoolbook of true wisdom.

Day 128
The Beauty of Holiness

Give unto the LORD the glory due unto his name:
bring an offering, and come before him:
worship the LORD in the beauty of holiness.
1 CHRONICLES 16:29

Holiness is true beauty, not what I wear or how my hair is done or how white my teeth shine. Indeed, holiness is Yours, never mine. I am fatally flawed, but I worship One who is perfect in all ways, One whose glory alone is worthy of praise and thanksgiving. There is no beauty compared to Yours, no faithfulness like Yours. The little glimpses of beauty that decorate my life are grains of silver sand at the edge of an incomprehensible ocean of beauty. I only see a grain or two in my lifetime, but it dazzles my eyes and makes me turn away blinking. I worship You in the beauty of Your holiness.

Day 129
Jesus' Redemption

In Him we have redemption through
His blood, the forgiveness of sins,
according to the riches of His grace.
EPHESIANS 1:7 NKJV

How glad I am, Lord, that my forgiveness doesn't depend on me, but on Your Son, Jesus. His grace gave me new life in You. When I could never have a perfect life on my own and I desperately needed Your forgiveness, Jesus' blood bought my soul. His redemption made me new from the inside out.

Help me live in Your redemption, Lord. I don't want to ignore Your great forgiveness or the change it has made in my life. Every good thing in me is there because of You.

I praise You, Lord!

Day 130
His Perfect Word

"As for God, his way is perfect:
The LORD's word is flawless;
he shields all who take refuge in him."
2 SAMUEL 22:31 NIV

If I want to know just what You're like, Lord, I need only look in Your Book. The scriptures are perfect, just like You, and show me how to live a life that's faultless in You. With Your Book in my heart and mind, I grow in faith and Your grace. Without Your guidance and advice, I'll never become the person You designed me to be.

Thank You for writing down for me all Your commands and guidance so I can take constant refuge in Your truth. With it, You shield me from sin and give me grace to live well.

Day 131
Spiritually Gifted

*Now to each one the manifestation of
the Spirit is given for the common good.*
1 CORINTHIANS 12:7 NIV

I know, Lord, I'm not the only Christian with spiritual gifts. You give them to each believer, and I need to recognize and respect the gifts of my brothers and sisters. Give me discernment and help me appreciate others' abilities so we can use them together for Your kingdom. We need to work together, not fight over who has the "best" gift.

Instead of becoming proud and self-righteous, I want to use my gifts to benefit my Christian family. Everything I do should benefit others, not just myself. So teach me how to use all You've given me to Your glory alone.

Day 132
Raised to New Life

We were therefore buried with him through baptism into death in order that, just as Christ was raised from the dead through the glory of the Father, we too may live a new life.
ROMANS 6:4 NIV

Such an amazing idea is hard to take in, Lord. Through baptism, which identifies me with You, I am raised up, just as You raised Your Son, Jesus, from the dead. My sins remain behind, and my life is new.

Help me to live this new life to glorify You, keeping ever before my face the truth that sin is behind me. I don't want to remain in the old place, when You've gifted me with so much that's fresh—and infinitely better.

Keep me faithful in Your new life, Lord. Each day may I walk beside You.

Day 133
Unsaying Words

*If any man among you seem to be religious,
and bridleth not his tongue, but deceiveth
his own heart, this man's religion is vain.*

JAMES 1:26

My email has an option to mark a message "unread." Although I don't personally utilize this feature, I do wish for an "unsay" option for my mouth. I am often dismayed at what I say and regret that the words cannot be taken back.

Lord, I pray that I will put my mind in gear before putting my mouth in motion. Instead of causing division and hurt, let my words uplift and bless. I pray that my conversations will bring unity and hope.

Day 134
Material Wealth

Let your conversation be without covetousness; and be content with such things as ye have: for he hath said, I will never leave thee, nor forsake thee.
HEBREWS 13:5

Dear Lord, You know I worry about money. Not because I am afraid I will not have enough, but because of my concern for those who depend upon me. I feel a strong obligation to provide for my family.

Lord, prevent me from using my role as a provider to rationalize an excessive devotion to making money. I pray that I will never measure success by material wealth or possessions. Thank You for assuring me that You will provide for my needs.

Day 135
Spiritual Poverty

But grow in grace, and in the knowledge
of our Lord and Saviour Jesus Christ.
To him be glory both now and for ever. Amen.
2 PETER 3:18

Father, I am struck by the fact that despite living in a wealthy nation, citizens with an inferior education may live as if they were in an underdeveloped country. Often I fail to understand that this principle applies to my spiritual life as well.

Lord, I am blessed with so many ways to delve deeply into Your Word. The Bible is available in both paper and electronic form. Bible dictionaries and other aids for studying scripture abound in many editions. Dedicated teachers conduct Bible studies tailored to the level of my expertise. I pray, dear Father, that I will take advantage of the opportunities to have a world-class spiritual education so that I will escape the poverty of spiritual ignorance.

Day 136
A Sense of Wonder

*Ye are our epistle written in our hearts,
known and read of all men.*

2 CORINTHIANS 3:2

Lord, Your Word is a light that guides me to righteousness. It contains wonderful poetry and soul-stirring songs. I read in it exciting stories of heroes of the faith. I marvel at its miraculous events, almost beyond human comprehension. Each day of reading the Bible is a new adventure and a wonderful journey.

I pray, Father, that I will always have a sense of wonder when I read Your Word, that it will always be fresh and illuminate my life. I pray that I will read Your Word, contemplate Your message, and keep it in my mind throughout each day.

Day 137
Humility versus Pride

But he giveth more grace. Wherefore he saith, God resisteth the proud, but giveth grace unto the humble.

JAMES 4:6

When the world makes pride look good, Lord, remind me that Your grace is for the humble. I turn aside from many "pleasures" in this world with a sigh, thinking I've lost out on something; but Your Word reminds me that those who resist You and Your will are the real losers.

Thank You for offering grace in increasing amounts. Encourage me in humility, that I may draw closer to You.

Day 138
Groanings Which Cannot Be Uttered

Likewise the Spirit also helpeth our infirmities: for we know not what we should pray for as we ought: but the Spirit itself maketh intercession for us with groanings which cannot be uttered.

ROMANS 8:26

Some days it's hard to pray, Father. I need Your guidance because I hardly know where to begin, let alone what to say or how to say it. Even when I have no special needs or requests and just want to praise You for all my blessings, I have a hard time finding the "right" words.

When that happens, I am thankful for Your Holy Spirit, who knows exactly what I want to say and intercedes on my behalf when my tongue fails me. Thank You, Father.

Day 139
God's Strength

*The LORD is my rock, and my fortress,
and my deliverer; my God, my strength, in whom
I will trust; my buckler, and the horn of my
salvation, and my high tower. I will call upon the
LORD, who is worthy to be praised:
so shall I be saved from mine enemies.*

PSALM 18:2–3

My Father, my strength, and my Redeemer, I cannot save myself from all that terrifies me. I cannot save those who love me and look to me for protection. The world presses in on me and defeats me, despite my best efforts, until finally I call on You for help and find You there, just waiting for me to ask. Great are Your powers, O Lord; great is Your mercy; great is Your love.

Day 140
A Broken Spirit

A merry heart doeth good like a medicine:
but a broken spirit drieth the bones.
PROVERBS 17:22

If a broken spirit dries the bones, Lord, about now mine should be dust. I'm not at all content with my situation, and my heart is down in the dumps. Turn my spirit toward You again, where I can find the joy and contentment I'm missing. May I feel Your Spirit touch my heart so that I may bring good to those I see each day. Help me rejoice in You, no matter what is going on in my life. I don't want sin to turn me into a pile of dry bones, and I don't want to share that attitude with others. Pour Your blessed balm on my aching heart, O Lord.

Day 141
The Work of Our Hands

And let the beauty of the LORD our God
be upon us: and establish thou the work
of our hands upon us; yea, the work
of our hands establish thou it.

PSALM 90:17

What I do for a living can be either secular or sacred. The choice is mine. The kind of work I do is not important. I can do anything in a way that glorifies You, Father. A worker in the humblest of jobs is just as capable of demonstrating Your beauty as one in the most exalted of positions. The next time I am feeling unproductive or unappreciated, remind me that I am working for Your glory, not my own. A tiny bit of Your beauty is reflected in my work, whatever it might be. May those I work with always see You in my life and be brought closer to You through me.

Day 142
Bearing Fruit

Herein is my Father glorified, that ye bear much fruit; so shall ye be my disciples.
JOHN 15:8

When I was called to be Your disciple, Lord, my first thought was for my own salvation. A great weight had been taken off my shoulders; You promised me many things I wanted and needed. All I had to do was accept what You offered. I was pretty selfish about my salvation. I finally realized that my soul had another purpose: to glorify the Father who had accepted me because of Your sacrifice. Whatever fruit my life was to bear would be a song of praise. Keep me mindful of this responsibility throughout my life, Lord. All I am and do should point the way for others, that they also can enjoy the benefits of salvation and join their voices in praise of Your Father in heaven.

Day 143
Getting Lost

*I will instruct thee and teach thee
in the way which thou shalt go:
I will guide thee with mine eye.*
PSALM 32:8

I am easily lost, Lord. My sense of direction is terrible, and maps just confuse me. On days before important appointments, I go out and see if the roads I know take me where I want to go, which usually means I get lost two days in a row. I certainly need Your guidance on the road. Of course I need it in more important matters too. Thank You for Your promise to guide me in all things great and small. Your eye is always on me, keeping me from error and ensuring that I can always find my way home to You no matter how often I wander off the right road or face detours and dead ends.

Day 144
Sin Forgiven

*"Blessed is the one whose sin
the Lord will never count against them."*
ROMANS 4:8 NIV

Before I knew You, Lord, I could not understand the blessings of forgiven sin. But Your Spirit's cleansing and the freedom that followed faith are more wonderful than I could ever have imagined. Nothing the world offers can take their place.

Thank You for not counting my sin against me, but instead sending Your Son to take my place on the cross. If You'd left me to pay the price for my own wrongs, new life would have been impossible. But because You've put my sin away from me, everything's changed. Your pardon affects every corner of my being.

I'm totally blessed by Your forgiveness, Lord. Thank You from the bottom of my soul.

Day 145
Jesus' Friends

*"You are my friends if you
do what I command."*
JOHN 15:14 NIV

Friendship with You, Lord, should mean the most to me. When I run out the door to be with another friend, I shouldn't leave You behind. Wherever we go, You can be a welcome third, who enjoys and blesses our fellowship.

Whatever I do, help me remember that Your friendship means more than any human relationship. I can't share with others the way I can with You; I'd never tell anyone else all the secrets of my heart. No one knows me as You do, even when I don't understand myself.

What You command, Lord, I want to do, whether I'm with others or alone. Help me and my friends to obey You always.

Day 146
God's Honesty

"And he who is the Glory of Israel will not lie, nor will he change his mind, for he is not human that he should change his mind!"
1 SAMUEL 15:29 NLT

How glad I am, Lord, that I can trust You not to lie or change Your thinking. You follow through on every promise, and nothing ever alters Your perfection.

You want me to be honest because that's what You are; and as I grow in You, I must increasingly reflect Your nature. Help me to become completely reliable. When I tell a friend I'll help out, I want him to be able to count on me. When a coworker needs the truth, let her be able to turn to me.

Every day, make me more like You, Lord. In my own strength, I'm only human; but Your Spirit makes me ever more like You.

Day 147
Christ's Body

Now you are the body of Christ,
and each one of you is a part of it.
1 Corinthians 12:27 NIV

You promise us that as Christians we are part of Your body, Lord. That's something I have a hard time understanding. But I know it means each believer is so firmly connected that not one can be separated from You.

When I disagree with a brother or sister, help me to remember that. I can't pull a person out of Your body or deny the salvation You alone can give. Though I don't understand another Christian's purpose in Your kingdom, I don't have the right to deny what You have done.

Help me live graciously with other members of Your body, Jesus, because I don't want to hurt them or You.

Day 148
Light's Power

The light shines in the darkness,
and the darkness can never extinguish it.
JOHN 1:5 NLT

Your light will never be extinguished, Lord. No evil or power of Satan can overpower Your strength. No depraved man overcomes Your will. Nothing wicked conquers Your love, power, and wisdom.

Remind me of that truth when overcoming sin seems hard. Instead of thinking that I have to overcome, I must remember I have no such ability. Nothing in me pierces the darkness; only Your power pushes back Satan's murkiness and brings me into Your pure light.

Without Your light, I'm lost, Jesus. Fill me with Your brightness, and use my life to do Your work of eradicating the darkness in the world around me.

Day 149
Being with Believers

I was glad when they said unto me,
Let us go into the house of the LORD.
PSALM 122:1

Heavenly Father, reading the Bible, talking to You in prayer, singing hymns, and meeting with other Christians help fortify my spiritual life. Only by becoming strong in You can I overcome obstacles. I need to assemble with other Christians because I gain strength from associating with those who love You. Our singing, praying, and study of Your Word inspire me to a closer walk with You.

Heavenly Father, I need the fellowship of dedicated believers. Help me realize that they need me too, because we are blessed through fellowship with others.

Day 150
A Gift from God

Give, and it shall be given unto you....
For with the same measure that ye mete
withal it shall be measured to you again.
LUKE 6:38

Lord, You set the standard for generosity by giving up Your life for a sinful world. May I always be reminded of Your sacrifice when I see a need that I can fill. Just as a farmer plants seeds and profits from the harvest, You also bless those who share their assets.

Heavenly Father, help me to give out of a pure motive to bless those in need, not out of a selfish expectation of reward. I truly want to act as Your hand extended to help those who have physical, spiritual, and financial needs.

Day 151
Praise in the Assembly

To appoint unto them that mourn in Zion, to give unto them beauty for ashes, the oil of joy for mourning, the garment of praise for the spirit of heaviness. . .that he might be glorified.

ISAIAH 61:3

Thank You, Lord, that in Your wisdom You have given me Your day as a reminder to rest and renew. As I assemble with other believers, the stresses of the week dissipate. I feel Your living Spirit as the unified body of Christ worships You.

I thank You, Lord, for allowing me to be a part of the assembly, where the cares of the week are put aside. There is joy in my heart as I leave Your house. Fellowship with other believers ignites a fire that burns in my heart throughout the week.

Day 152
Victory over the Giant

David said moreover, The LORD that delivered me out of the paw of the lion, and out of the paw of the bear, he will deliver me out of the hand of this Philistine.
1 SAMUEL 17:37

Dear God, I work out in a gym; but despite my efforts, I will probably never be as strong as some of the other people there who work out.

Mighty Lord, I am happy that You do not require physical strength to do battle for righteousness. You helped young David defeat Goliath with just one stone and a sling because he trusted You to be his deliverer. Likewise, I offer You my faith with the understanding that You will make it powerful enough to conquer situations regardless of how hopeless they may seem.

Day 153
Worthy of Honor

*O LORD our Lord, how excellent
is thy name in all the earth!*

PSALM 8:9

O Lord, I have peered into a microscope and seen a world in one drop of water. I have gazed through a telescope and have seen stars and galaxies uncountable. When I see the majesty of Your vast creation, I am brought to my knees in wonder. But in my humble admiration, there is also a desperate question: Do You notice me and concern Yourself with me?

I thank You, Lord, for personally answering my question. When I am apprehensive, I put my trust in You, and You keep me safe. When I am lonely, You talk to me. When I am sad, You make me happy. When I am weak, I bow before You and feel Your strength.

Day 154
Dynamic Leadership

Stand therefore, having your loins girt about with truth, and having on the breastplate of righteousness; and your feet shod with the preparation of the gospel of peace.

 EPHESIANS 6:14–15

Father, when I am called upon to be a leader, I sometimes feel that I am not the one best equipped to lead. Grant me the capacity to confront this apprehension and overcome it. When making decisions, may I always listen to others so they will gladly participate in our common goal. Equip me to follow Your guidance and direction so that I select the right course of action.

I know that my leadership may not be universally accepted. Let me be unflinching in carrying out my work, despite criticism. May I lead by example and with a humble attitude.

Day 155
"Fret Not"

Fret not thyself because of evildoers,
neither be thou envious against the workers of
iniquity. For they shall soon be cut down like the
grass, and wither as the green herb.
PSALM 37:1–2

Thank You for Your promise, Lord, that tells me that even the most wicked people cannot take the world out of Your hands. Before cold spiritual weather withers their hearts, may I reach out to evildoers with Your Good News. Let none be cut down or wither because I would not share the contentment I find in You.

Day 156
Believing without Seeing

*Whom having not seen, ye love;
in whom, though now ye see him not, yet
believing, ye rejoice with joy unspeakable
and full of glory: receiving the end of your
faith, even the salvation of your souls.*

1 PETER 1:8–9

I am one of Your peculiar people, Lord, set apart from the world by both my beliefs and my actions. I have never seen even Your sandal prints at the edge of the lake, yet I follow You with all my heart. My ears have never heard Your voice, but I live by Your words. My fingertips have never brushed the edge of Your garment, yet I am healed. My belief is not based in my senses or my intellect but in Your never failing love, which saved my soul and promises me unspeakable joy.

Day 157
Separation

Behold, what manner of love the Father hath bestowed upon us, that we should be called the sons of God: therefore the world knoweth us not, because it knew him not.

1 John 3:1

The world doesn't understand what it means to love You, Lord. Sometimes I feel that truth very deeply when I witness to a friend and he looks at me as if I were strange. When a coworker just can't understand why doing right matters to me, I can feel awfully odd.

But I would rather be at Your side than on the side of all those who don't love You. They don't know me because they don't know You, not because I am strange. Let the difference You make in my life shine out through me.

Day 158
A Witness

By this shall all men know that ye are
my disciples, if ye have love one to another.
JOHN 13:35

Lord, I have to admit that loving my brothers and
sisters in Christ can be hard. I tend to get caught
up in what my "siblings" are doing and how I feel
about it. Your promise that love will be a witness
to the world sometimes seems impossible.

But how I feel about it doesn't change Your
command to love. I know I can't love on my own;
but through Your Spirit I can do all things—even
this. When I seek to love others, I need to keep
my eyes on You, not their flaws. Sweep away my
critical attitude, and fill me with Your love.

Day 159
Faithful

A friend loveth at all times,
and a brother is born for adversity.
PROVERBS 17:17

Thank You, Lord God, for the faithful friends who have stood by me in adversity. Sometimes they seem more like brothers or sisters than my own siblings do. When that happens, my friends and I know it's because Your love fills our hearts. Thank You for giving me such relationships.

I too want to be a friend at all times, the way my friends have been to me. Help me choose my friends wisely and stand by them when they need encouragement or help. When life challenges their faith, I want to be standing right at their sides.

Day 160
Mustard Seed

If ye have faith as a grain of mustard seed,
ye shall say unto this mountain, Remove
hence to yonder place; and it shall remove; and
nothing shall be impossible unto you.

MATTHEW 17:20

A grain of mustard seed is so small it's nearly invisible. How could anyone who loves You not have at least that much faith? And yet even Your disciples failed from time to time because of unbelief.

This is a great mystery to me, Father. Some days my faith is so strong I can almost see it. I'm not quite up to moving mountains, but I feel Your power within me, and I dare to believe I am capable of anything. Other days, my faith seems puny and weak. Be with me on both my strong and weak days, because no matter how I feel, I want to do Your work.

Day 161
Unworthiness

If we confess our sins, he is faithful and just to forgive us our sins, and to cleanse us from all unrighteousness.

1 John 1:9

On my worst days, I feel totally unworthy. I gather up my little pile of sins like dirty laundry and shake them toward the sky. "How can You possibly forgive this sin?" I ask, repeating the process until all my sins have been displayed. On my best days, I calmly confess my sins (the exact same sins I had the day before), accept Your forgiveness, and go on with my life without guilt. I suspect that both reactions to guilt are acceptable, however. Confession is confession no matter how I phrase it. You have promised to cleanse me from all unrighteousness, to wipe away my guilt and make me whole if I confess my sins, and I thank You on both my good and bad days.

Day 162
The Promise Fulfilled

And the LORD visited Sarah as he had said,
and the LORD did unto Sarah as he had
spoken. For Sarah conceived, and bare
Abraham a son in his old age, at the set
time of which God had spoken to him.
GENESIS 21:1–2

You promised that Abraham would be the father of many nations and You would be their God forever. You would give them the land of Canaan as an everlasting possession and never leave them as long as they obeyed Your commands. But before Abraham could be the father of nations, he needed to father a son—not the son of a servant, but Sarah's son, whom You had chosen. And so it was. We cannot begin to understand how Your promises are fulfilled, Father; but we know nothing is impossible for You, and all Your promises will come true. All we need is faith.

Day 163
The Peace of God

*And all thy children shall be taught
of the LORD; and great shall be
the peace of thy children.*

ISAIAH 54:13

A child that accepts You as her Savior possesses an inner peace that no army can ever guarantee, Lord. Turmoil is part of our life on earth, and children sometimes have much to worry about, much to fear from others. But a child who clings to You knows a special peace that overcomes all fears. The victory has already been won, and she has nothing to fear being in the hands of her Savior. This knowledge is the greatest gift I can pass on to my children. I have the faith that overcomes, and I wish this blessing for them. Help me teach all our children about You, about Your great promises, and about the peace that I pray will be their inheritance.

Day 164
My Guide

For if ye forgive men their trespasses,
your heavenly Father will also forgive you.
MATTHEW 6:14

I need to be forgiven for my sins, Father; they are many, and they keep me from fellowship with You. But if I have to forgive those who have deeply hurt me, I find I have a real problem. I can say the words, "I forgive my sister for what she said," but in the back of my mind I hear, "No, I can't. Not really." I don't want to add lying to my sins, so what can I do? I need Your help, Father. By myself, I cannot truly forgive some wrongs, but Your strength is sufficient. Show me the way to true forgiveness, I pray. I want to do Your will despite my weakness. Be my guide along this difficult path that leads to my own sorely needed forgiveness.

Day 165
Jesus, the Overcomer

*"I have told you these things, so that in
me you may have peace. In this world
you will have trouble. But take heart!
I have overcome the world."*
John 16:33 niv

When I face the enemy, Jesus, I can still have peace. Not in my ability to withstand sin in my own strength, but in Your ability and willingness to overcome everything evil that I face today.

No trouble I face is beyond Your command, Lord. Whether it's at home, on the job, or in the community, there's no place I go that You won't go with me. As I face evil, I never stand alone. I don't have to rely on my strength alone to get me through.

Thank You, Jesus, for overcoming all the trials and troubles in my life. When You overcome, I too am wholly victorious.

Day 166
Judgment

The wicked will not stand in the judgment,
nor sinners in the assembly of the righteous.
PSALM 1:5 NIV

Right now it's hard to see the truth of this scripture. Wicked people don't seem to be punished, and they stand right next to believers, sometimes acting as if they shared the same faith. It's discouraging, Lord, not to see them receiving the justice I know they deserve.

But I'm glad that things won't always be this way. I can trust in Your promise that when Judgment Day comes, those who never followed You will receive their reward too—and it won't be a nice one. In heaven there will be none of the confusion that's on earth about who really knows You and who just pretends.

But I also ask, Lord, that You would turn many to You. After all, there was a time when I was wicked too.

Day 167
Self-Discipline

For the Spirit God gave us does not make us timid, but gives us power, love and self-discipline.
2 TIMOTHY 1:7 NIV

As You grow my faith, Lord, You've made me aware that serving You shouldn't be a hit-or-miss thing—an option among others—but my life goal. Every choice I make should boldly work to forward Your kingdom, not my own self-interest.

I don't have to take that bold stance alone. Even when I lack strength to do the right thing, to make a choice that will be good for many days instead of just one, You help me decide well. When I'd like to go for the short-term benefit, Your Spirit reminds me I'm not only living for today—there's eternity to consider.

In You I have a spirit of power, love, and the self-discipline that obedience requires. Help me to live faithfully only for You, Lord.

Day 168
Self-Control

A person without self-control is
like a city with broken-down walls.
PROVERBS 25:28 NLT

Though self-control doesn't seem very appealing, Lord, You promise that the person who lacks it will be like an unwalled city, defenseless in the face of opposition. So many things attack me in my spiritual life that I don't want to forgo any defense.

Though controlling my tongue when I'd rather speak my mind or doing the right thing when a sin is tempting may not thrill me, Your Word shows me it's the only way to be secure in You. So give me the ability to bite my tongue or stand up for what's right, even if it isn't popular. Help me always to do Your will instead of what feels good today.

Day 169
At Mealtime

And God said, Behold, I have given you every herb bearing seed, which is upon the face of all the earth, and every tree, in the which is the fruit of a tree yielding seed; to you it shall be for meat.

GENESIS 1:29

I praise You, living God, who made all things. You spoke into existence the plant and animal kingdoms. You created a people in Your image to take care of Your creation.

Thank You, Lord, for the fruitful seasons that are made possible by Your design—the seasons of seedtime and harvest. I see eternity in the seeds of each fruit and vegetable because they ensure a harvest year after year. For the blessings of the dinner table, whether a simple staple like bread or a hearty main course, I give You praise, O Lord.

Day 170
Setting Goals

He hath shewed thee, O man, what is good;
and what doth the LORD require of thee,
but to do justly, and to love mercy,
and to walk humbly with thy God?
MICAH 6:8

Father, last year a friend and I set out to hike a mountain trail. We had no particular destination in mind. The grueling trail ended in a field of boulders and an impassable bank of snow. Later we learned of a different route that would have taken us to a spectacular vista at the summit.

Father, I often expend my strength to reach an unworthy goal. No matter how effective I am, if I do not first select a worthy goal, the end result will be disappointing. In my walk with You, I pray that I select the right goal and always keep it firmly before my eyes.

Day 171
Refreshment

Nevertheless he left not himself without witness, in that he did good, and gave us rain from heaven, and fruitful seasons, filling our hearts with food and gladness.
ACTS 14:17

Father, as a young child on a farm, I viewed rainy days with pleasure. My outdoor chores were put aside, and I could devote a few hours of time to my special interests. Afterward, I would return to my chores with renewed vigor. As an adult, I sometimes view rain with less enjoyment. I become exasperated if I must change my plans. But even as I find rain an unwelcome inconvenience, I recognize it as an essential part of nature.

Heavenly Father, help me recognize that the difficulties in my life are like rain. The interruptions to my routine give me opportunities to refresh my spirit.

Day 172
The Real Article

But the wisdom that is from above is first pure,
then peaceable, gentle, and easy to be intreated,
full of mercy and good fruits,
without partiality, and without hypocrisy.
JAMES 3:17

Father, years ago a coworker sold me a gold ring. After a hot and sweaty day, my skin under the ring had turned green. The ring was not pure gold but had only gold plating over copper.

Lord, I pray that my character is not a veneer on the outside. Instead, may the way that I appear on the outside flow from within. Through deliberate effort, I want to develop the attributes—honesty, honor, hospitality, and humility—from which character springs. Father, ensure that the words I say, the actions I take, and the thoughts of my heart are an indivisible combination that reflects a life dedicated to You.

Day 173
The Gospel

*And he said unto them, Go ye into
all the world, and preach the gospel to
every creature. He that believeth and
is baptized shall be saved; but he that
believeth not shall be damned.*

MARK 16:15–16

Faith in other things won't save me, Jesus. You commanded Your disciples to preach to the entire world because only faith in You will bring anyone to faith.

I'm so glad that someone told me the Good News that You came to save me. Thank You for that messenger who helped me understand my need. I want to pass on the same message to others who have never heard it. Open my lips and provide the words that will share Your truth with many.

Day 174
Service without Fear

That he would grant unto us, that we being delivered out of the hand of our enemies might serve him without fear, in holiness and righteousness before him, all the days of our life.

LUKE 1:74–75

Enemies come and go throughout my life. Some are serious dangers that require Your supernatural protection; others You allow me to handle with Your guidance. What have I done to deserve such protection?

I have tried to serve You in some form or another, and You want me to be free to continue that service. You protect my back so my energy and actions are available for Your work.

Thank You for Your love and care, Lord. May my life reveal Your holiness and Your power so others may come to worship You too.

Day 175
A Change of Heart

The Lord is gracious, and full of compassion;
slow to anger, and of great mercy.
PSALM 145:8

O Lord, how I wish I too were slow to anger. I confess I'm too quick to say harsh words or hand out condemnation.

If You treated me the way I sometimes treat others, I would be in deep trouble. How glad I am that compassion and graciousness are the hallmarks of Your attitude toward me. Help me have that attitude toward others.

Lord, take this anger from me and make me more like You. Increase the flow of mercy in my life. I want to be just like You, Jesus.

Day 176
Serial Sinning

And if he trespass against thee seven times in a day, and seven times in a day turn again to thee, saying, I repent; thou shalt forgive him.
LUKE 17:4

Some people are just like little children who never seem able to avoid mischief, Lord. They trip their brother and apologize, then run off to sock their sister, all the time saying, "I'm sorry, Mommy. I'm sorry." I'm not much better, Lord. I shake off one sin, repent of it, then run right into another, all the time claiming, "I'm sorry. I'm really sorry." And I am sorry every time—just as my child is, just as my neighbor is. My only hope is in You, whose patience is perfect. If You can forgive me, surely I can forgive my child or my neighbor, no matter how many times forgiveness is required. Thank You, Lord.

Day 177
Dying in Hope

The wicked is driven away in his wickedness:
but the righteous hath hope in his death.
PROVERBS 14:32

The life we have lived can be a great comfort to those we love when it comes time for us to die. They have enjoyed our love; they have witnessed our good deeds and seen the evidence of our faith. They are secure in the knowledge that we are with You even as they mourn. They do not fear for our soul, and that lifts a great weight from their minds. Even in death, we comfort them. Teach me to live this kind of life, Lord. Let me leave those I love in peace, not fear. It has been my pleasure to ease the burdens of those I love, and I would like to do so one last time by living and dying in hope.

Day 178
Varieties of Strength

In returning and rest shall ye be saved;
in quietness and in confidence
shall be your strength.

ISAIAH 30:15

The strength of women is not the same as the strength of men. In times of danger, it is usually the men who arm themselves and rush out to defend their own through the use of force. Women make their own preparations for trouble, storing away food and water, seeing there is enough clothing for all, preparing the children for bad news. Men's strength is loud and brash; women's is quiet and confident in the Lord. Of course this is a generalization. Some women fight; some men stay at home as rocks of faithfulness.

Lord, remind me that there are many legitimate ways to respond to danger. If I choose to fight, grant me Your protection. If I choose to serve in another way, in quietness and confidence in Your mercy, that too is strength.

Day 179
Being There

Cast me not off in the time of old age;
forsake me not when my strength faileth.
PSALM 71:9

There comes a time in every person's life when their parents—those strong, loving people who gave their all to raising their children—will begin to need help. When that time comes for me, Father, give me the wisdom to understand the problems my parents are having and the often simple ways I can be of service to them. Show me how to make time for them in my busy life now, to give them what they need and want the most—my love and attention, time with their grandchildren, and my promise that I will never forsake them. Above all, Father, help us find the suitable balance between independence and protection that will assure their safety and maintain the dignity they so deserve.

Day 180
Correction

Stern discipline awaits anyone who leaves the path; the one who hates correction will die.
PROVERBS 15:10 NIV

Lord, I don't enjoy being corrected, whether it comes from You or from another Christian. I'd rather believe I always do the right thing—but that isn't so. The truth is that to stay on Your narrow path, I need direction from You and wise believers.

Though I don't want to hear correcting words or experience those hard-hitting moments when I know I'm wrong, I know I need them. They seem unpleasant now, but they keep me from falling into greater error and missing Your way entirely.

Help my spirit be gentle enough to accept correction, even when it hurts. I know You only mean it for my benefit. And if I have to correct another Christian, let it be with a kind and righteous spirit.

Day 181
Finding Life

"Whoever finds their life will lose it,
and whoever loses their life
for my sake will find it."
MATTHEW 10:39 NIV

The new life You promise, Lord, isn't simply for a few years—not even one hundred of them. Your life lasts forever, and I will share eternity with You. That's why You tell me not to cling too closely to this world. Eternity doesn't depend on my going with the crowd here on earth, because their choices don't last. It doesn't require that I please anyone but You.

I want to use this life to make a difference for eternity. In the here and now I can share Your love with those who don't yet know You and those who struggle to live their new lives well. Whatever I lose in this world, let it be for gain in Your kingdom.

Day 182
Suffering

"Do not fear any of those things which you are about to suffer. Indeed, the devil is about to throw some of you into prison, that you may be tested, and you will have tribulation ten days. Be faithful until death, and I will give you the crown of life."
REVELATION 2:10 NKJV

Not fearing suffering seems impossible, Lord. Suffering is not something any Christian looks forward to, yet all of us experience it in some way. Still, I know You have brought faithful believers through much more than I've experienced.

I haven't been imprisoned for my faith, Lord; but You promise You'll be there even if that should happen. Then if I stay faithful for a short time, I'll receive Your eternal crown of life and rejoice with You in heaven.

No matter what I suffer, keep me faithful to You, Jesus. I don't want anything to harm our relationship.

Day 183
Worthy of Hire

The labourer is worthy of his hire.
LUKE 10:7

No matter what kind of work I do, You provide me with a way to live, Lord. As You provided for those first-century Christians who went out to preach Your Gospel, You want me to be supported. Even those who do Your work need a way to live.

But whether I labor in a factory, in an office, or preaching Your Good News, You know all my needs. Whomever my work blesses, that person or group should help me have enough to live on. No one can live on nothing.

But I also want to do my best for those I work for. Let me be worthy of my hire by always giving an excellent effort. Then I will shine for Your kingdom.

Day 184
Quality Friendship

*One who has unreliable friends soon
comes to ruin, but there is a friend
who sticks closer than a brother.*

PROVERBS 18:24 NIV

Having too many companions seems like a funny problem to have, Lord; but You're saying that many of these folks aren't really friends. Some people simply like to play at friendship when they can benefit from it.

Having a friend who sticks closer than a brother is wonderful, Lord. I know I always have Jesus, my best friend; but I also know what it's like to have Christians who've become so close they seem nearer than blood family. Your kingdom friendship, which lasts eternally, means more than a fair-weather friend or an uncaring sibling.

Help me stick closer than a brother to my Christian siblings. I know some have faithless brothers or sisters—and they may need to borrow one from Your family.

Day 185
Sacrifice of Praise

*By him therefore let us offer the sacrifice
of praise to God continually, that is,
the fruit of our lips giving thanks to his name.*
HEBREWS 13:15

Lord, my life has been relatively devoid of the kinds of sacrifices made by Christian pioneers of the past. What sacrifices can I make?

Heavenly Father, I sacrifice to You my self-will. To the one and only living God, I submit my life as an offering of worship. Another sacrifice I offer is one of praise. Purify my mouth that my praise may be acceptable to You. I give thanks for Your redemption. All praise, honor, and glory belong to You.

Day 186
Independence Day

And ye shall know the truth,
and the truth shall make you free.
JOHN 8:32

Heavenly Father, summer travel brochures always seem to show a person strolling along a white sandy beach, lying in a hammock, or watching a sunset. My vacations aren't as leisure filled; and by the time they are over, I look forward to returning to work. Independence Day is my favorite summer holiday because it lasts only one day—a backyard barbecue, a ball game, evening fireworks, and it is over.

Thank You, Lord, for my personal independence day, the day You broke me away from sin so I could begin a personal, daily association with You as my guide.

Day 187
For Government Leaders

I exhort therefore, that, first of all,
supplications, prayers, intercessions,
and giving of thanks, be made for all men;
for kings, and for all that are in authority;
that we may lead a quiet and peaceable
life in all godliness and honesty.
1 Timothy 2:1–2

Heavenly Father, I ask that You guide the leaders of my country. May they have integrity, morality, and leadership ability. Guide them to extend Your influence into all areas of society. Empower them to overcome the dark forces at work in the world.

Father, I ask for Your guidance upon my government's leaders. Direct them to take our nation in the way You would have us go. Help them realize that true prosperity comes only through the application of Christian values. May the laws they make uphold and protect our right to worship You.

Day 188
Nothing New

*I have seen all the works that are
done under the sun; and, behold,
all is vanity and vexation of spirit.*
ECCLESIASTES 1:14

Each day, Lord, I am bombarded with advertisements. Embedded in the glittering generalities is the assurance that the merchandise is on the leading edge. The fashion models are chosen because of their appeal to the young and vigorous. I suddenly discover a product that is essential, although I have been getting along without it all of my life. I disparage as outdated my perfectly serviceable possessions.

Heavenly Father, I pray that I will not allow advertisements to exploit my tendency to be discontented. Help me dismiss sales pitches that appeal to desire and pride. Keep me away from the idea that I can improve my future with *things* rather than by living for You.

Day 189
Coals of Fire

If thine enemy be hungry, give him bread to eat;
and if he be thirsty, give him water to drink:
for thou shalt heap coals of fire upon his
head, and the LORD shall reward thee.

PROVERBS 25:21–22

Lord, my natural reaction to anger is to make life harder for my enemies, not easier. Not many people would offer to cook a steak dinner for a hungry burglar before sending him off with the silverware. Any enemy certainly would be taken aback by such a response. He might even feel guilty and ashamed.

You tell me I am to treat everyone—even those who hurt me—with love and concern, and You will reward me for my actions. The next time I am prepared to lash out at someone who has hurt me, let Your forgiveness and love be reflected in my response.

Day 190
God's Provision

The young lions do lack, and suffer hunger: but they that seek the Lord shall not want any good thing.
Psalm 34:10

Gracious Lord, thank You for Your faithfulness in providing for those who follow Your way righteously. I know every creature of this earth will face difficult times sooner or later. Even the strong may go hungry, but You are faithful to meet my needs.

When You have blessed me by Your provision, remind me to share the blessing with others less fortunate than I am, so they will have the strength to continue in the faith through my generosity. Help them see that Your provision may come in many forms, from many sources, but every good thing ultimately comes from You.

Day 191
Eternal Life

*Search the scriptures; for in
them ye think ye have eternal life:
and they are they which testify of me.*

JOHN 5:39

Father, eternal life comes no other way but by knowing Your Son, Jesus. Thank You for providing Your Word as a testimony to Him, for from it I learn the truth about Your love for me and the sin that separates me from You.

When questions arise in my heart or the hearts of those who do not believe in You, make me quick to search Your Word for the evidence of truth. Keep me daily in the scriptures so that I will always be ready to respond to doubt.

Day 192
Uncertain Riches

*Charge them that are rich in this world,
that they be not highminded, nor trust in
uncertain riches, but in the living God,
who giveth us richly all things to enjoy.*
1 TIMOTHY 6:17

Heavenly Father, compared to the rest of the world, I am rich and living a good life. My basic needs are being met, and I have an abundance of funds. Keep me mindful of my blessings, no matter how much or how little I have. Encourage me to use what I have in a way that brings glory to You. Riches can fade away in the blink of an eye; only You remain faithful forever.

Day 193
Correcting in Love

Children, obey your parents in the Lord:
for this is right. Honour thy father and
mother. . .that it may be well with thee,
and thou mayest live long on the earth.
EPHESIANS 6:1–3

Even young children have responsibilities, but You carefully pair every command with a promise—a tactic that most parents readily learn. This is not bribery but cause and effect; children who obey and honor their parents find family life far more enjoyable than those who don't. Then You add a second promise that can only come from You: "and thou mayest live long." Raising obedient, loving children requires me to show gentleness and patience, not threats or harshness. I pray that You will teach me how to soften each correction with the same love I receive from You, who guides and corrects me. May Your patience and kindness be made visible through my actions.

Day 194
Laborers with God

For we are labourers together with God:
ye are God's husbandry, ye are God's building.
1 CORINTHIANS 3:9

The best thing about working is knowing I'm not working alone. I may plant the seeds, but You water them. I may do the weeding, but You send the sunshine. All I am and all I do is done with You, the One who created me and gifted me with whatever skills I have. You give my work—whatever type of work it may be—dignity and purpose. Your faith in me enables me to continue my duties on days when I would otherwise despair. At the end of the day, my feet may be burning, but I know I am walking in Your footsteps, and that gives me peace. I thank You for the work I have. May I do it in a way that is pleasing to You and reflects Your glory.

Day 195
A Seat at the Table

Use hospitality one to another
without grudging.
1 PETER 4:9

Hospitality involves an effort, whether it's a big party or throwing another potato in the stew for an extra dinner guest. Hospitality means greeting newcomers after church services, maybe giving them the name of a good babysitter or pizza place. It means going to my child's piano recital and applauding every child, not just my own. It is doing little kindnesses cheerfully.

Lord, You welcomed me into Your family with love and acceptance. I was not worthy of Your hospitality, but You found me a seat at the table and fed me with Your Word. Help me be as kind to others as You have been to me—joyfully welcoming everyone who wishes to dine with me tonight.

Day 196
Hope in Trouble

But God will never forget the needy;
the hope of the afflicted will never perish.
PSALM 9:18 NIV

I certainly have needs, Lord. They often overwhelm me until I hardly know where to turn.

But I still hope in You, Jesus. I know You will never forget me or desert me, and You will always provide a way out of my troubles. No matter what problems we have faced, You have never yet forgotten or given up on Your people. Though it may take some time, You faithfully respond.

In my need, assuage my physical and spiritual emptiness, Lord. Without Your Spirit's flow in my life, I am still afflicted. I trust in hopeful restoration through You—fill me, Lord.

Day 197
God's Coming Judgment

*Then shall the trees of the wood sing
out at the presence of the LORD,
because he cometh to judge the earth.*
1 CHRONICLES 16:33

I don't often think about joy and Your judgment in the same moment, Lord. Too many people who don't know You make me think of things other than how wonderful Your return will be. Right now, I focus more on reaching out to those who have yet to come to You in faith.

But one day, the entire earth will rejoice as You take control of the world that has always been Yours. The time for accepting You will be past, and You will judge according to the choices we've already made. Then I will sing with the trees of the forest and the rest of the earth. How wonderful to see my Lord in whom I've believed!

Day 198
Putting on Christ's Image

You have put off the old man with his deeds,
and have put on the new man who is
renewed in knowledge according to
the image of Him who created him.
COLOSSIANS 3:9–10 NKJV

Lord, I'm being renewed, according to Your promise. As I grow in knowledge of You, I become more like You every day.

Some days I don't feel much like You, Lord, when I struggle to do Your will. But other days, I begin to see the changes You've made in my heart. I rejoice in that new me. But I ask You: help me not to become proud about the reconstruction and give myself the credit. I know only You could make these heart alterations.

In all things make me into Your image, Lord. I need the change so much.

Day 199
Faithful God

*And those who know Your name will
put their trust in You; for You, LORD,
have not forsaken those who seek You.*
PSALM 9:10 NKJV

Anyone who knows Your name—Your
character—will trust in You, Jesus. What more
could You sacrifice for us than Your life? And
that gift of salvation was designed to benefit us.

When I think about Your faithfulness to Your
people, I can't fathom it. So often, we swerve in
our belief. Distractions and temptations pull us
far from You. Yet You have not given up on us,
even when we would give up on ourselves. I
know You've kept me seeking, even when Your
way seemed difficult to find.

Thank You for Your continued love and trust,
Lord. Keep me doing Your will all my days.

Day 200
Dangerously Dead

Trust ye in the LORD for ever: for in the LORD JEHOVAH is everlasting strength.
ISAIAH 26:4

Lord, the great oak tree had become danger-ously dead, but no one could tell. The death was in the heartwood, working from the inside out. When the storm came, the trunk snapped, fell, and crushed some smaller trees nearby.

Father, sometimes I become enamored with people that I consider towering Christians. But I cannot see their hearts, and occasionally their lives collapse because they have become only a shell of Christianity. When they fall, I become disillusioned.

Father, I pray that Satan does not destroy those individuals who are in the public eye. I pray also that my trust will always be in You as my unfailing leader.

Day 201
Fully Armored

*Put on the whole armour of God,
that ye may be able to stand
against the wiles of the devil.*

EPHESIANS 6:11

Father, when I first gave my life to You, I hungered for Your Word. Every day I read the Bible and studied it carefully. Now my mind strays as I read, and I have to double back and reread passages to comprehend them. I question how much my mind retains and wonder what benefits I am receiving. Yet, each day I eat meals so my body has food to repair tissues and provide energy for physical activities.

In the same way, I understand that reading Your Word provides food for my soul. Lord, I pray that I will always be so hungry for Your Word that I will set aside time for daily Bible reading.

Day 202
Spiritual Vitamins

*My people are destroyed
for lack of knowledge.*
HOSEA 4:6

Heavenly Father, my doctor told me a dietary deficiency was causing the skin to flake off my fingers. Despite robust meals, some essential component was missing from my diet. The doctor recommended that I consume more fish each week to provide the missing ingredient, and the problem disappeared.

Father, if I search through Your Word and read only those passages that I find most agreeable to my preconceived ideas of Your message, then I am missing some of the essential elements that I need for a strong relationship with You. I pray that I will choose to become healthy by accepting all the spiritual vitamins that You have provided me in Your Word.

Day 203
Destroying Darkness

For the commandment is a lamp;
and the law is light; and reproofs
of instruction are the way of life.
PROVERBS 6:23

Dear Father, every time I replace a light bulb, I wonder why it burned out so quickly. Regardless of its limits, I am thankful for light that expels darkness.

Lord, because You used the example of light throughout scripture, I am able to understand Your holy character and comprehend the power that You have to destroy the darkness of sin. Jesus, let Your light shine through me so others will be exposed to the heavenly light that You delivered to earth long ago. I pray for Your guidance in my effort to share Your light with the lost world.

Day 204
Worldly Possessions

But thou shalt remember the LORD thy God: for it is he that giveth thee power to get wealth, that he may establish his covenant which he sware unto thy fathers, as it is this day.
DEUTERONOMY 8:18

I don't think of what I have as wealth, Lord; it isn't enough to buy out a major corporation. But You've given me enough to fulfill Your covenant. You've cared for me every day of my life. I haven't appreciated enough how You've taken care of me or the way You have kept me going, even in rough times.

You've also given me countless spiritual blessings: a church to worship in, Christian friends, and Your love.

Thank You for the spiritual and financial wealth You've given me. I want to use it to Your glory. Show me how to spend it for You this day.

Day 205
The Lord Enables

*And I thank Christ Jesus our Lord, who hath
enabled me, for that he counted me faithful,
putting me into the ministry.*
1 TIMOTHY 1:12

Lord, on my own, I am not capable of doing
Your work as a preacher or evangelist. The life
is hard, and I am weak. But You take me as I am
and mold me into an individual capable of more
than I ever imagined. Only You know my talents
and abilities and call me to the type of service
best suited for me. Forgive my doubts and fears
and show me where I am needed, that Your will
shall be done.

Day 206
Blessings

*For the LORD hath redeemed Jacob, and
ransomed him from the hand of him that
was stronger than he. Therefore they shall. . .
flow together to the goodness of the LORD. . .
for the young of the flock and of the herd:
and their soul shall be as a watered garden;
and they shall not sorrow any more at all.*
JEREMIAH 31:11–12

How many blessings You have heaped on me,
Lord. Not only do You provide me with physical
things; my spirit feels Your goodness. My soul
flourishes, like a well-watered garden carefully
tended by Your hand. You nourish my life and
make it fruitful.

All my blessings flow out of Your salvation,
Father. How can I thank You enough for Your
love and care each day of my life? I can only offer
my heart to You in obedience.

Day 207
Dealing with Guilt

I, even I, am he that blotteth out
thy transgressions for mine own sake,
and will not remember thy sins.
ISAIAH 43:25

Sometimes, Father, I find myself striving for perfection, certain that I can live a holier life if I only work on myself a little more. Of course what happens is that I make progress on one particular sin at the expense of working on another and end up tormented by guilt.

Remind me that this is not a victory I can ever claim for myself. Sin is with me and will always be with me. Yet You promise that You will not even remember my sins because You choose not to! You sent Your Son to deal with my sin, and the job has been done. This is not a do-it-yourself project. Thank You, Father.

Day 208
Our Source of Strength

*The righteous also shall hold
on his way, and he that hath clean
hands shall be stronger and stronger.*
JOB 17:9

On my own, I am rarely as strong as I need to be, Lord. Sickness weakens me; cares and worry tire my mind and make me less productive than I want to be. Old age will eventually defeat my body. Even when I am physically fit, I know there is weakness in me. But You promise that I will be able to continue in Your way as long as I have faith and I trust Your promises. Make me stronger every day, Lord, no matter how heavy my burdens may be. Show me all the good You have done for the faithful throughout history, and give me some of Your strength when my own fails. Let my dependence on You turn weakness into strength.

Day 209
The Reward

Then shall thy light break forth as the morning, and thine health shall spring forth speedily: and thy righteousness shall go before thee; the glory of the LORD shall be thy reward.
ISAIAH 58:8

You promise me wonderful rewards when I am charitable, Lord. I will be "like a watered garden, and like a spring of water, whose waters fail not" (Isaiah 58:11). Good health will come to me, as well as good reputation; and I will live a life of righteousness. Remind me of this the next time I pass up a charity event for an evening in front of the television or hang up the telephone without even listening to the caller. I cannot answer every request made of me, so I count on You to guide me as to where I should invest my efforts in such a way as to bring You glory.

Day 210
Judgment

The wolf also shall dwell with the lamb,
and the leopard shall lie down with the kid;
and the calf and the young lion and the fatling
together; and a little child shall lead them.
ISAIAH 11:6

Children are easily frightened by the prospect of judgment. They know they have sinned just as we, their parents, have and feel anxiety about their accounting, even though they have accepted their salvation through You. You gave us this verse to reassure us. Who would be afraid to live when the hunters and the hunted live together in perfect peace? There will be no more wars, no more politics, no more fear, only Your righteous rule forever. "And a little child shall lead them." When my children ask about Your coming, remind me of this promise so they will not fear what should be a great day for us all.

Day 211
Redeemed by God

*The LORD redeems the soul of His
servants, and none of those who
trust in Him shall be condemned.*
PSALM 34:22 NKJV

You bought me out of sin, Lord, though I still struggle to make that truth complete in my life. I may attempt to completely understand this change, but it's beyond my finite mind. I recognize that You did not purchase only a portion of my life, but the whole thing—and every day You make me more like You. Thank You for giving me Your redemption in place of Satan's condemnation.

Help me to trust in You whenever I fall into sin. I need to know You care and still want to make me whole. Let my heart become tender to Your touch, and may I quickly confess all wrong. Then I can experience the peace You offer my soul.

Day 212
Hurt by a Friend

Wounds from a friend can be trusted,
but an enemy multiplies kisses.
PROVERBS 27:6 NIV

When a friend hurts me, it cuts deeply, Lord. But I'd rather hear the truth about myself from someone who loves me than listen to the lies of an enemy. People who hate me can't hurt me much, but they also can't help me by showing me places where I need to grow in You.

Open my heart to painful truths told by one who cares. Aid me in sifting what's said, to know which words are right and which might be off base; and help me forgive a friend who offers well-meant but mistaken critiques.

When a hurt comes directly from You, Lord, I want to be humble enough to accept it and profit from it. In the end, You are my best friend, who cares more than I can ever truly understand.

Day 213
Renewed Strength

But those who hope in the LORD will renew their strength. They will soar on wings like eagles; they will run and not grow weary, they will walk and not be faint.
ISAIAH 40:31 NIV

What a soaring promise this is, Lord God, one all Your people treasure.

I've needed this promise, Lord, when work—for You or on the job—seemed too hard. I've wanted to soar, run, and walk for miles when my strength has been small and my heart has been heavy. You've empowered me to do that. Though the way may have been hard, You've given me energy to go on and prosper.

Your promise has already brought me strength in trials, but I know there's a lot more soaring to do. I want to finish my life in Your power and reach for eternity too.

Day 214
Righteousness and Anger

*Human anger does not produce
the righteousness that God desires.*
JAMES 1:20 NIV

Could You make it clearer, Lord? I don't think so. When I am angry, I'm not righteous. No matter how hard I try, I can't make anger do Your will because it's against everything You stand for.

So help me, instead, to control my emotions. When I see a wrong done, I know You don't want me to ignore it; but You want me to handle it calmly and in faith that You can work even in this. I need self-control to hold on to that truth when my emotions run high.

Even when the fire of anger licks at my soul, I want to remain strong in You. Let my responses always reflect Your desires, not my own.

Day 215
Defeating the Enemy

*"Behold, I give you the authority to
trample on serpents and scorpions,
and over all the power of the enemy,
and nothing shall by any means hurt you."*

LUKE 10:19 NKJV

Often, I don't feel much like an overcomer, Lord.
Temptation feels very real, and too often I fall
into sin. But You look at my spiritual history differently. You see the long haul, both the future
and the past; You see the end of my life, as well
as the beginning.

You're promising me victory in the end. As
I walk faithfully with You, You give me an increasing ability to say "no" to sin. The serpents
of temptation fall beneath my feet and no longer
harm me.

Nothing hurts me forever when I walk with
You, Lord. Keep me strong in clinging to You
alone.

Day 216
God's Justice

*"Have nothing to do with a false charge
and do not put an innocent or honest person
to death, for I will not acquit the guilty."*
EXODUS 23:7 NIV

When sin harms an innocent person, it's easy to wonder where You are, Lord. "Why did this happen?" I ask. "Why wasn't it stopped?"

Verses like this give me hope, though. You warn Your people not to do evil because You will not acquit them. How much less will You acquit someone who has no regard for You or relationship with You.

When I can't see Your justice, help me still to trust in it. Let me know a response is on its way, even if You don't show it before I meet with eternity.

Day 217
Individuals Matter to God

So we, being many, are one body in Christ,
and every one members one of another.
ROMANS 12:5

Lord, as a child I would stand over an anthill and watch ants go about their business. I marveled at their ceaseless effort. Yet, it bothered me that each worker ant was not clearly different from the others.

I rejoice that I have a unique personality. As a Christian, I have strengths and weaknesses. I have talents for some tasks but must depend upon others to carry out those jobs that I cannot do. I am Your gift to others—and they are Your gift to me. Dear God, help me use my individual abilities to share Your love with others.

Day 218
Hope

*And Joshua said unto them, Fear not,
nor be dismayed, be strong and of good
courage: for thus shall the Lord do to all
your enemies against whom ye fight.*
JOSHUA 10:25

Father, sometimes I become despondent. My outlook becomes gloomy. It is as if some of the light has gone out in my life. Yet, such a feeling would only be justified if I were without hope. And that is certainly not the case. Your love, the grace of Jesus Christ, and the guidance of the Holy Spirit are with me.

Father, help me face the challenges before me with boldness. Give me strength to shake off anything that troubles my mind so that I can press on each day with a clear purpose. Help me ignore any troubling concerns that might slow my steps.

Day 219
The Growth of Sin

*Then when lust hath conceived,
it bringeth forth sin: and sin, when it
is finished, bringeth forth death.*
JAMES 1:15

Dear Lord, during a visit to the Everglades, I saw a larger tree that was being slowly strangled by a fig tree. Months earlier a bird dropped a tiny fig seed that lodged in the bigger tree's branches. The fig tree sprouted and began sending its roots earthward, spiraling around the host tree. Eventually the death-hug of the fig tree will prevail and destroy its host.

Father, I often ignore sinful practices until they become dangerous to my spiritual life. For sin to flourish, it must be nourished by the very person it is harming. May I be ever alert to sin's influence and rely on Your help to conquer it.

Day 220
A Song of Praise

The LORD is my strength and my shield;
my heart trusted in him, and I am helped:
therefore my heart greatly rejoiceth;
and with my song will I praise him.

PSALM 28:7

I sing to You, O Lord, a continual song of praise. I declare Your name to all those who come into my presence. Words of thanksgiving are forever upon my lips. I can sing a new song because of Your grace and power. Your holy name is exalted in heaven and on earth, O Lord Most High. Your righteousness causes my heart to rejoice and break forth in a song of praise: "Glory to the God of my salvation. The generosity of Your compassion overwhelms my soul."

Day 221
God's Protection

*Behold, all they that were incensed against thee
shall be ashamed and confounded:
they shall be as nothing; and they that strive
with thee shall perish. Thou shalt seek
them, and shalt not find them.*
ISAIAH 41:11–12

Father, You have promised the righteous Your protection from their enemies. They may still come against me, but they will be powerless, ashamed, and confused by their inability to harm me. Your power against them is so fearsome that when I search for my enemies, I will not be able to find them.

Such protection is beyond my understanding but not to be taken lightly. You know exactly what I need when I call on You for help; and I trust Your decisions, especially when I am in fear for my life. Thank You, Father.

Day 222
God's Blessings

But godliness with contentment is great gain. For we brought nothing into this world, and it is certain we can carry nothing out. And having food and raiment let us be therewith content.

1 TIMOTHY 6:6–8

I have much to be thankful for, Lord. You have given me a family that loves me, a job that puts food on my table, a place to sleep in safety, and clothing to keep me warm. I have the necessities of this life and Your promise of the life to come.

Forgive me when I ache for a little more, especially for my spouse and children. I know You want the best for me, and You will provide it. My job is to live my life in a way that glorifies You. Everything beyond that is an extra blessing. I choose to be content.

Day 223
My Reactions

*If ye endure chastening, God dealeth
with you as with sons; for what son
is he whom the father chasteneth not?*
HEBREWS 12:7

You are my perfect Father, but I am Your imperfect child, full of human failings and sometimes in need of correction. If You did not love me, You would ignore my misdeeds, leaving me to my own devices and letting the chips fall where they may; but You do not do this. You love me and therefore correct me, as I do with my own children.

Like my children, I do not always welcome correction. I pout; I avoid You; I try to go my own way. I even say, "It's not my fault!" as if I were not responsible for my own actions. In times like these, be patient with me, Father, because I cannot live without Your love.

Day 224
Contact with the Unsaved

*Blessed is the man that walketh not
in the counsel of the ungodly,
nor standeth in the way of sinners,
nor sitteth in the seat of the scornful.*
PSALM 1:1

You promise to bless me, Lord, when I turn away from constant contact with evil people. Help me glorify You through my friendships and associations. But continue to keep my heart burning to reach those souls who do not know You. May my prayers remain constant, asking that Your Spirit would touch the souls of the unsaved around me. My prayers can still reach out to those with whom I do not walk, stand, or sit.

Turn their lives around, just as You have mine.

Day 225
My Self-Condemning Heart

For if our heart condemn us,
God is greater than our heart,
and knoweth all things.
1 John 3:20

Guilt? I know it well. It lives in my heart and tries to convince me that You could never love me as much as You love far better people. My heart tells me I barely have a passing grade and should forget the honor roll. No singing for me in heaven; I'll probably be polishing silver and gold all day.

But You are greater than my heart, Father; and when my heart is wrong, it doesn't fool You. You know everything that was and everything that is yet to be. You forgive my sins and make me far better than my self-condemning heart thinks I am. Rid me of my useless guilt. I would be honored to polish Your silver for eternity.

Day 226
Dealing Wondrously

And ye shall eat in plenty, and be satisfied,
and praise the name of the LORD your God,
that hath dealt wondrously with you.
JOEL 2:26

You promised to do great things for Israel, Father, even more than You did for them in the past, when You brought them out of Egypt. You would defend them from attack and restore the fruitfulness of the soil, enriching them and guaranteeing them good lives. "The floors shall be full of wheat, and the vats shall overflow with wine and oil" (Joel 2:24). Frightening events would soon take place, but whoever called on the name of the Lord would be delivered. "The LORD will be the hope of his people, and the strength of the children of Israel" (Joel 3:16).

Through turmoil and fear, You always protect and save those who love You. You will provide; You will save.

Day 227
A Child in the Crowd

And he took a child, and set him in the midst of
them: and when he had taken him in his arms,
he said unto them, Whosoever shall receive one
of such children in my name, receiveth me.
MARK 9:36–37

In biblical times, young children were not considered much use until they could contribute to the family's welfare. Yet You reached through the crowd of adults, including the disciples, and pulled a little child into Your arms as an example of faith. This must have surprised the child, who had undoubtedly been jostled and shoved away by the crowd. He may not have seemed important to the adults, but You knew the importance of childlike innocence and faith. Salvation lies along that path. I know my children have much to teach me, Lord. Help me be receptive of Your lessons, especially when You send them through a child.

Day 228
The Empty Wastebasket

As far as the east is from the west,
so far hath he removed our
transgressions from us.
PSALM 103:12

It's good to know You keep no "permanent file" with my name on it, Father. It would take up a lot of space. Like a good businessperson, You only handle a piece of paper once: read it, act on it, toss it. Or in more biblical terms, hear my confession, forgive me, then wipe away my sins forever. Toss them in a basket on the far side of the world and burn the contents of the basket every night. I'll surely be back tomorrow with another load.

Thank You for dealing with my sins so thoroughly, Lord, for granting me a new start every day and proclaiming that while I am worth saving, my confessed sins are not.

Day 229
Light of the World

*"You are the light of the world.
A town built on a hill cannot be hidden."*
MATTHEW 5:14 NIV

You left a light in this wicked world, Lord—and it's me. That's a scary thought because I don't like to think that without my witness, Your work on earth could be less effective.

I know You call millions of people to Your work, and Your light cannot be hidden forever, but no one else is in my spot. Could my place be a critical one in the work You are doing?

I want to shine brightly for You, Jesus. You promise my light cannot be hidden, but it might burn faintly. I'd rather illuminate as much of my world as I can, Lord. Help me do just that.

Day 230
Everlasting Truth

*"The grass withers, and the flowers fade,
but the word of our God stands forever."*
ISAIAH 40:8 NLT

So much changes in life, Lord. Just when I think I'm secure, I can almost count on some fluctuation, and my world becomes different again. Just as the seasons alter and the flowers die off, life is constantly moving.

But Your truths aren't one thing in the summer season and another in fall. Your Word doesn't say one thing this month and something new ninety days later. It always shows me what You are like and never changes. I can count on scripture always to be truthful and to lead me in the right path.

Thank You, Lord, for sharing Your everlasting truth with me. Help me to be steadfast in clinging to Your way.

Day 231
Feeling Far from God

But if from there you seek the Lord your God,
you will find him if you seek him with all
your heart and with all your soul.
DEUTERONOMY 4:29 NIV

Sometimes when I hurt, I feel so far from You, Lord, that I begin to wonder if You even care anymore. When I experience that feeling, often it's because the world has gotten in between us. I've fallen into sin, and the sin looks good. Or I've let being overly busy keep me from time with You. Forgive me, Lord.

A life off course becomes a lonely existence. Even in a crowd, I feel far from everyone. All I need to do is return to You. Turn my heart again in the right direction, Lord. Help me put aside all that divides us and draw close to Your side again.

Day 232
Overcomer's Inheritance

"He who overcomes shall inherit all things, and I will be his God and he shall be My son."
REVELATION 21:7 NKJV

I'm humbled, Lord, at this promise. I know You already call me Your child, but the thought that You'd provide me with this kind of generous inheritance—all things—just blows me away. I know You love me, but how amazing the depth of Your love seems.

Yet, Lord, how could I imagine that You'd be less than completely generous? Your nature isn't anything else, and I've experienced it over and over in my own life. Could You do any less than overwhelm me with Your blessings in eternity?

Most of all, though, I look forward to our eternal relationship of God and loved child. Anything less than this, it couldn't be heaven.

Day 233
For Boldness

And in nothing terrified by your adversaries:
which is to them an evident token of perdition,
but to you of salvation, and that of God.
PHILIPPIANS 1:28

Dear Lord, each day I encounter people who have chosen to walk a path that conflicts with Your laws and those of our government. Their goals are contrary to honest living, and they identify me as their adversary. I pray for fearlessness born of confidence in Your protection as I confront evil.

Father, You give me boldness greater than my natural ability. I walk by Your side, and with Your strength I overcome the fear of what others might do to me. Help me develop strength of spirit, physical courage, and the intelligence to rightly employ these when they are required.

Day 234
A Ready Harvest

Pray ye therefore the Lord of the harvest, that he will send forth labourers into his harvest.
MATTHEW 9:38

Father, even from my limited gardening experience, I've seen that weeds grow without encouragement, but good crops require attention. Seeds must be planted in soil that has been prepared to receive them, weeds must be eliminated, and produce must be harvested at the right time.

Almighty Savior, I see that the same sequence is necessary to produce a spiritual harvest. Lord, make me a faithful worker in Your harvest. Help me to be diligent in the work that brings the lost to You. May I have an urgency to gather souls into Your kingdom before the season is past and the crop is lost.

Day 235
Righteousness

And the LORD said unto Noah, Come thou and all thy house into the ark; for thee have I seen righteous before me in this generation.
GENESIS 7:1

Lord, sometimes I look around and see all kinds of sin in this world. I let my guard down, and I am tempted to say or do something I know is wrong. In moments like that, I remember the account of Noah. He refused to compromise his righteous walk with You, Lord. The evil people of his day mocked him as he built the ark, but You honored his righteousness by saving him and his family from the flood.

Dear God, help me to find favor in Your eyes by maintaining Christian traits. The most important concern in my life is to please You.

Day 236
Comfort of the Holy Spirit

But the Comforter. . .shall teach you all things,
and bring all things to your remembrance,
whatsoever I have said unto you.
JOHN 14:26

Lord Jesus, just before You ascended into heaven, the disciples wondered what would happen to them after You went away. You told them that You would send the Holy Spirit to be their Comforter and Teacher. By Your power they were able to boldly spread the Good News throughout the sinful world.

Today, Lord, I want to thank You for the gift of the Spirit working through Your children. I trust Your power to give me joy and hope. Produce spiritual fruit in my life, and pour Your love in my heart by the Holy Spirit.

Day 237
Waiting at the Door

I am come a light into the world,
that whosoever believeth on me
should not abide in darkness.
JOHN 12:46

Lord, so many people stumble through life in darkness, afraid of what they might touch in the blackness, of what they might become. They have no sense of direction and no peace in their lives; only anger and fear keep them moving.

You stand outside the door, life-giving light in Your presence, if only they would turn the key and welcome You. You will wait there forever, if need be, eternally patient and loving. I pray they will hear You knocking on their hearts; may they gather up their courage and answer Your call, for You offer them light, guidance, and nothing less than salvation itself.

Day 238
Walking in Wisdom

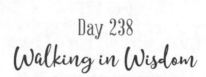

And he will teach us of his ways,
and we will walk in his paths.
Isaiah 2:3

You have promised me that I can know Your ways and walk in them, Lord. What a blessing that is to me, for I cannot know You more closely unless I know how You want me to live and how to follow in Your footsteps.

I may not always be sure of my path. But I can be sure of You; as I continue to seek Your way, You will lead me to the right goal.

You, Lord Jesus, are always my goal. You are the end of my path; my eternal reward is to live with You forever. Thank You for leading me to Your eternal home.

Day 239
Brotherly Love

Beloved, let us love one another: for love is of God; and every one that loveth is born of God, and knoweth God. He that loveth not knoweth not God; for God is love.
1 John 4:7–8

Thank You for the reminder that love is a three-way street, Lord. It doesn't simply depend on me and my brother or sister, but on You as well. Whatever my relationship, You have a part in it. I cannot fail to love a fellow Christian and not fail to love You.

You have promised that those who love are born of You. I don't want to act like someone who has never known Your love or healing power. Bring Your love into each relationship I have, and let it be a testimony to Your ability to bring love into humble human lives. Fill my life with Your outreaching love.

Day 240
God's Forgiveness

For the LORD your God is gracious and
merciful, and will not turn away his
face from you, if ye return unto him.
2 CHRONICLES 30:9

How far I have strayed from Your commandments, Lord. It hurts to know how I've harmed
You and those I love.

You've promised that if I return to You, You
will not turn away. Forgive my sin, Lord, and
help me make things right with those I've hurt.
Help them to forgive my wrongs too.

Turn my heart from evil, Jesus, and help me
be more like You each day. Put this sin in my
past—forever.

Day 241
Waiting for the Reward

Let not thine heart envy sinners: but be thou in the fear of the LORD all the day long. For surely there is an end; and thine expectation shall not be cut off.
PROVERBS 23:17–18

Sometimes I wonder, Lord: Why do sinners seem to flourish while Your people struggle to support their families? Is it better for me to be poor? Surely there are those better off than I who are righteous; couldn't I be one of them? I get tired and discouraged.

But You promise that all bad things come to an end; my heart's desire will one day be mine. Until then, give me contentment with the blessings I have and faith in tomorrow.

Day 242
Prayer Warriors

Confess your faults one to another,
and pray one for another, that ye may
be healed. The effectual fervent prayer
of a righteous man availeth much.

JAMES 5:16

There are prayer warriors all over the world who pray daily for the health of everyone suffering or in need, whether they know them personally or not. They do their work totally without fanfare, sometimes as a group, often individually. If I have confessed my sins and been forgiven, somewhere someone will be praying for me, even if in a general way. I won't even know I am in their prayers and may never suspect that my healing has come through them. Bless these prayerful, unselfish people, Lord. Reward them for their efforts on behalf of all believers who are ill, and assure them that their efforts are not in vain.

Day 243
God's Promises Are Sure

He hath given meat unto them that fear him:
he will ever be mindful of his covenant.
PSALM 111:5

Father, being human, with human weaknesses, we may forget our promises to our children, but You never forget Your promises to us. You remain honorable and full of compassion even when we are weak and easily frightened. Your commandments stand forever, as does the redemption of Your people through Jesus Christ. Out of Your great mercy, You will always provide for those who love You and follow Your ways. Remind me of this when I am in need of food or shelter, Lord. Sometimes my needs seem to be the most important things in my life, but I know this is only panic speaking. I need never panic again: Your promises are sure. Help my desperation of today give way to Your reassurance and love.

Day 244
The Promise

*For the promise is unto you, and to your
children, and to all that are afar off, even
as many as the LORD our God shall call.*
ACTS 2:39

Peter was surrounded by people asking what
they must do to receive the Holy Spirit. His answer was simple: "Repent, and be baptized. . .
for the remission of your sins" (see Acts 2:38).
This promise was given to all, from every nation,
of every status, near or far, adults and children
alike. You will do the calling; all we need do is
repent and be baptized. The process is simple
so that even the simplest can understand. Help
me explain this to my children, Lord. I yearn
to know they belong to You, for, as John said, "I
have no greater joy than to hear that my children
walk in truth" (3 John 4).

Day 245
Persistent Prayer

"Ask, and it will be given to you; seek, and you will find; knock, and it will be opened to you. For everyone who asks receives, and he who seeks finds, and to him who knocks it will be opened."
MATTHEW 7:7–8 NKJV

I've asked for things in prayer and not gotten them, Lord. Then I've started to wonder if I should have asked at all. But this verse encourages me not only to ask once, but to seek and knock persistently for the good things of Your kingdom.

When I don't get an immediate answer, Lord, remind me to check with You to make sure my request is good—and then to keep on trusting and persisting. You don't ignore my prayers, even if I don't get the response I'd wanted. You will answer when the time is right.

Thank You, Lord, for Your answers to every prayer.

Day 246
Anxiety Cure

*Cast all your anxiety on him
because he cares for you.*
1 PETER 5:7 NIV

What do I need to worry about when You are in charge of my life, Lord? Nothing in this world is greater than You.

But I do get concerned about the things I face. When money's running short or a relationship isn't going well, I can get so agitated that it's almost as if You weren't in my life anymore. I know that's not true because You promised never to leave me—but I can certainly act as if it were so.

Remind me when worry attacks that I need only to cast every care on You. You will resolve everything better than I ever could. Thank You, Jesus, for loving me so much.

Day 247
Possibilities

*All things are possible
to him that believeth.*
MARK 9:23

What an amazing promise this is, Lord! I can hardly believe You wrote this to me. You've opened so many doors to me simply because I have faith in You.

I know that amazing promise does not mean I can demand anything I want. There are plenty of wrong things in this world—or things that would simply be wrong for me—that Your promise doesn't automatically cover. But You have given me an open door to all the good things You offer me, all the positive things that I can do, and all the challenges You want me to overcome.

When it comes to the things You say are right, I don't want to think too small. All things are possible in You.

Day 248
Little Things

*Behold also the ships, which though they
be so great, and are driven of fierce winds,
yet are they turned about with a very small
helm, whithersoever the governor listeth.*
JAMES 3:4

Father, when I first came to You, I was so determined to do great works that I considered little jobs beneath my effort. When I fell short of my goals, I despaired of ever doing anything for You. All along, a multitude of small deeds have been available, but I ignored them.

Lord, grant me eyes to see tasks that need to be done and a willing heart to do them. In Your name, I ask Your help in using my daily activities to show kindness and concern for others.

Day 249
Living Words

And thou shalt teach them diligently unto thy children, and shalt talk of them when thou sittest in thine house, and when thou walkest by the way, and when thou liest down, and when thou risest up.

DEUTERONOMY 6:7

Father, I know that You call upon me to teach my children Your law. It is easy for me to tell my children what to do if I think I do not have to do it myself.

Father, help me be like Jesus, who illustrated His powerful sermons with examples of love, compassion, and humility.

I want my children to receive good training by examples of my actions. May I demonstrate Your love in my daily routine. Lord, write Your commandments on my life so they will be a living lesson to my children.

Day 250
Emergency Response

The LORD is my shepherd; I shall not want.
He maketh me to lie down in green pastures:
he leadeth me beside the still waters.
He restoreth my soul.
PSALM 23:1–3

Father, the feeling of foreboding was upon me again. I knew that something awful was going to happen. So I came to You in prayer and read the Psalms. That time of meditation cleared the mental overcast. I saw that the day was bright and sunny, and the disasters I had imagined never occurred.

Father, help me keep the well of anxiety empty. Prevent me from refilling it by brooding over past events or imagining future disasters. Help me face the issues that cause my anxiety and build my response upon realistic assumptions. I will stay in touch with You so that I may look to the future with hope.

Day 251
Prejudice

Thou shalt not avenge, nor bear
any grudge against the children of
thy people, but thou shalt love thy
neighbour as thyself: I am the LORD.
LEVITICUS 19:18

Jesus, You have taught me that to live in heaven forever with You, I must be a good neighbor. Your parable about the Samaritan who offered aid shows that every person should be treated with kindness, even people who others might hate or despise because of their language, skin color, or place of birth.

Lord, so that I can live with You in heaven, give me the determination to act upon the truth that all people are equal in Your sight. Let me show kindness to everyone because all are created in Your image.

Day 252
Pages of Time

*Let not mercy and truth forsake
thee: bind them about thy neck;
write them upon the table of thine heart.*
PROVERBS 3:3

Lord, with my internet browser, I can specify the subjects that are displayed when I log on. I can choose the news content, weather report, financial statements, sports scores, and entertainment guide. I can build a personal page that is unique to me.

Father, today You have given me a fresh page of my life. I can write upon it words that encourage or words that destroy, acts of kindness or selfish deeds, thoughts that cause my spirit to soar or ideas that bring me low. Let me wisely choose the content of my life to glorify You.

Day 253
The Sacrifice

But that ye may know that the Son of man hath power on earth to forgive sins. . .arise, take up thy bed, and go unto thine house. And he arose, and departed to his house.

MATTHEW 9:6–7

There is absolutely no doubt that Your Son had total faith in You, Father. You gave Him the power to forgive sins and heal, and He did not hesitate to demonstrate Your glory through His healing. He must have known that His miracles would lead to suffering and death. Being truly human, He must have felt some fear because of what was to come, and yet He healed to show us that You had given Him the power to forgive sins, that all could be saved through faith, even though He knew that every healing brought Him closer to death. Thank You, Lord, for Your great sacrifice.

Day 254
Sanctification

*For the unbelieving husband is sanctified
by the wife, and the unbelieving wife
is sanctified by the husband.*

1 CORINTHIANS 7:14

Father, I believe that it is best for believers to marry other believers. Their goals are the same; their priorities agree; life generally has fewer conflicts. But love will have its own way, and sometimes believers love and marry nonbelievers. When this happens, I must assume You have a reason. Many unbelieving spouses have come to You through the good example of their loving partners—not through their preaching or nagging, but through the love they share and the kind of life that love makes possible. Let me not be quick to harshly judge such a marriage. Let me give love time to do its work. I may never see the result I want, but I am sure it is safely in Your hands.

Day 255
Without Wavering

*Let us hold fast the profession
of our faith without wavering;
(for he is faithful that promised).*
HEBREWS 10:23

Lord, with Your blood You wiped away my sins, leaving me promises to enjoy in faith until You come back again to claim me as Your own. It takes patience to live in faith, and I confess that sometimes my patience runs thin. I wonder why You don't act in ways that I can see and understand. Why is there so much evil and suffering in this world that discourage both the faithful and the unfaithful? I don't understand. Help me realize that my understanding is not necessary for the completion of Your plan. You understand everything; all I need to do is have faith. In the meantime, keep me free from wavering, Lord. Your faithfulness is perfect, and Your will is going to be done.

Day 256
The Person Within

For man looketh on the outward appearance,
but the LORD looketh on the heart.
1 SAMUEL 16:7

We are too conscious of outward beauty today, Lord. Our singers, our heroes, our role models— even our politicians—are expected to meet certain standards of beauty. Even worse, we instinctively trust the beautiful, never looking beyond their bodies, as though perfect hair indicates a perfect brain or a pure heart. When we stop to think about it, we know this is foolish, but we rarely do think about it. Make me more conscious of this error, Lord. Teach me to look through appearance when I choose my heroes or my spouse. A perfect hairdo should not unduly influence me—it may be warming a very small brain. An expensive Italian suit may very well be covering a dark heart. Help me see beyond beauty—or the lack of it.

Day 257
A Loan to God

*He that hath pity upon the poor lendeth
unto the LORD; and that which he hath
given will he pay him again.*
PROVERBS 19:17

Lord, You have given me an opportunity to give,
but I'm wondering if I can afford to do it. You
know my financial situation and the needs of
the future better than I do, yet I struggle with
this choice.

Thank You for making Your will clear by calling my heart to give and offering me this promise: if I loan money to You, I will never lose. I
offer my finances and future to You, knowing
You will provide for me.

Day 258
When Doing Right Goes Wrong

For the LORD knoweth the way of the righteous:
but the way of the ungodly shall perish.
PSALM 1:6

Sometimes, Lord, even doing right gets me into trouble. My heart seemed to be in the right place, but things didn't work out the way I expected. The good I thought would happen turned sour.

Thank You, Jesus, that even this situation is not out of Your hands. You knew what would happen even from the start, and the results are under Your control.

I know I can trust You to make all things right, even if it takes some time. Whatever happens, make me a good testimony to Your love.

Day 259
God's Faithfulness

There hath no temptation taken you but such as is common to man: but God is faithful, who will not suffer you to be tempted above that ye are able; but will with the temptation also make a way to escape, that ye may be able to bear it.
1 Corinthians 10:13

How glad I am that You gave me this promise, Lord. Even when temptation becomes sharp and compelling, I know You have provided a way out. If I flee from sin, You will lead me into freedom.

Help me avoid temptation when it is still very small, Lord. I don't want to allow things into my life that could draw me away from You.

Thank You for being an escape hatch that is constantly available. Don't let my pride keep me from freedom.

Day 260
Christian Suffering

For unto you it is given in the behalf
of Christ, not only to believe on him,
but also to suffer for his sake.
PHILIPPIANS 1:29

According to Your promises, Lord, suffering is part of the Christian experience. It's not one I enjoy; but to know You more completely, I must experience suffering. If I trust You and have lived out my commitment faithfully, I need not worry about suffering and ask where it comes from. Those who trust in You need have no fear.

Help me to deal with suffering in a way that draws others to You and brings glory to Your name. I want to be faithful in all things.

Day 261
My Thankfulness

Every man also to whom God hath given riches and wealth, and hath given him power to eat thereof, and to take his portion, and to rejoice in his labour; this is the gift of God.

ECCLESIASTES 5:19

It is truly a blessing when I am able to enjoy my work and the profits of that work, Father. While I may not be rich, I have much more than the rest of the world, and You allow me pleasures that are unknown to many.

When I turn from thankfulness and begin to desire some of the things I do not have, remind me of the millions who suffer in poverty every day, no matter how hard they work. Remind me of Your blessings that have little to do with wealth: love, peace, good health, and the work of the Spirit in my life. Remind me of the great cost of my salvation, and let me praise You forever.

Day 262
The Powerful Word

For the word of God is alive and powerful.
It is sharper than the sharpest two-edged
sword, cutting between soul and spirit,
between joint and marrow. It exposes
our innermost thoughts and desires.

HEBREWS 4:12 NLT

I've known what it's like to be cut by Your Word, Lord, and I can't say I always like what I read. I'm pierced, as with a knife, when You point out my intentional sin or a place where I've failed. Sometimes I'd like to run away from the pain. But escape won't offer me a changed life. Only if I listen to and obey Your Word can its power heal my soul. Your truths change me and guide me in the best path.

I need Your Word's power to cleanse me from sin, Lord. Change my heart and give me new wisdom as the scriptures fill my head.

Day 263
Overcoming Hardship

*You have allowed me to suffer much hardship,
but you will restore me to life again and lift
me up from the depths of the earth.*
PSALM 71:20 NLT

When life gets hard, Lord, I sometimes wish the hurt would end or that I could run away from it. Pressure doesn't feel good, and I simply want to escape. But even when I feel a lot of pain, remind me that none of it is out of Your control. Though I may not understand pain's purpose, You have allowed this into my life to create something good.

When I face hardship, help me through it—then restore me to life. Instead of leaving me in the valley, bring me up the mountainside so I can see Your plan anew.

Day 264
Heart Purity

Blessed are the pure in heart:
for they shall see God.
MATTHEW 5:8

When purity of heart, mind, and soul seems difficult, remind me of this promise, Lord. Seeing You is the greatest blessing I could receive—I especially long to look directly into Your face.

In this world, I cannot see You fully, though every day I perceive more of Your love, grace, and blessing as I draw nearer to You in obedience. I cannot see You physically, yet I get a clearer spiritual picture of You every day as I live out Your commands. Reading Your Word, praying, and acting in a way that pleases You make You ever clearer to my heart and soul.

Make my heart increasingly pure, Lord. Long before we meet face-to-face, I want to know You well.

Day 265
God-Caused Frustration

The eyes of the LORD keep watch
over knowledge, but he frustrates
the words of the unfaithful.
PROVERBS 22:12 NIV

Lord, I've been frustrated by a lot of things in my life, but I'm glad that as long as I follow You, I won't be frustrated by You. I can't imagine the pain I would face should You be against me.

Because I know You, You share Your knowledge with me, teaching me how to live successfully in the world You created. Because You know everything about the earth and about me, You offer the guidance I need.

I can't imagine trying to live on my own as one who doesn't know You. How painful life is for those who have never met You. Turn their pain to joy as they come to You in faith.

Day 266
Complex to Simple

I will greatly rejoice in the LORD, my soul shall be joyful in my God; for he hath clothed me with the garments of salvation, he hath covered me with the robe of righteousness, as a bridegroom decketh himself with ornaments.

ISAIAH 61:10

Father, I see the wonder of Your creation in all of its complexity, and I bow before You in humble adoration. When I study the world You have created, I cannot but admire how the complex parts work together as a simple whole.

When I read the Bible and study Your Word, it is at first a complex story that spans the ages. But then I see Your guiding hand behind the events that brought Jesus into this world, and I see how His death and resurrection give salvation to those who simply accept You by faith. I admire and honor You for giving me a simple salvation plan, one that I can comprehend.

Day 267
Responsibility

While we look not at the things which are seen,
but at the things which are not seen: for the
things which are seen are temporal; but the
things which are not seen are eternal.
2 Corinthians 4:18

Father, when I was young, some children would excuse their failures or belittle someone else's successes by saying, "In a hundred years, no one will remember this." Now, that comment allows me to contrast trivial and important matters. Significant comments and actions have a way of reaching beyond the present and affecting eternity.

Lord, let me never take lightly my responsibility to dedicate my words and actions to You. Use what I say and do to influence someone to seek eternity with You in heaven. Today I trust that I have done all I could for You.

Day 268
The Master's Voice

But be ye doers of the word, and not hearers only, deceiving your own selves.
JAMES 1:22

Dear Lord, I am thankful that You were kind enough to provide Your Word. The orderliness of nature tells me of Your existence; I would be miserable knowing that You had created me but then abandoned Your creation. I sense Your presence when I read the Bible. I hear Your voice and learn that You take a personal interest in me. Your Word gives me a glimpse of You.

Lord, I pray for the will to read Your Word, a mind to understand its meaning, the ability to apply its principles to my life, and the determination to act upon what I learn.

Day 269
Toward Eternity's Sunrise

*Therefore my heart is glad, and my glory
rejoiceth: my flesh also shall rest in hope.*
PSALM 16:9

Heavenly Father, during my morning drive to
work, the day is brighter and the air is cleaner
than it was when I drove home the night before.
Each sunrise brings a fresh day in my spiritual
life too.

Thank You, Lord, for releasing me from my
past failings so I can face the day with a glad
heart, secure in the knowledge that Jesus has
given me a new start. As I drive on to my destination during the morning rush, I also desire
to stay on the spiritual highway that leads to
my eventual destination with You.

Day 270
Dreadful Superstition

Regard not them that have familiar spirits,
neither seek after wizards, to be defiled
by them: I am the LORD your God.
LEVITICUS 19:31

Father, help me guard against falling into superstition under its many guises. I unfold and read a slip of paper with my fortune from a Chinese cookie, but I place no credence upon anything it says. I open the entertainment section of the newspaper and see the horoscopes for that day, but I push such nonsense out of my mind and turn the page.

Father, help me continue to ignore and avoid these and all other dreadful superstitions. My trust is not in fortune-telling but in You and Your Word.

Day 271
Driving on High Beam

Let your light so shine before men, that they
may see your good works, and glorify
your Father which is in heaven.
MATTHEW 5:16

Father, when I am driving in the country late at night, I am thankful to have the brilliant high-beam headlights to warn me of deer that might wander onto the road. The focused, concentrated light gives me advance warning of any dangers ahead of me.

Dear Jesus, You gave Your disciples the responsibility of living as lights to guide the lost to You. Let Your heavenly beams shine through my life to reveal You as the Savior of the world and to focus praise on the Father. Help me to be diligent in illuminating the narrow road that leads to heaven.

Day 272
Self-Help

"But the word of the LORD endures forever." Now this is the word which by the gospel was preached to you.
1 PETER 1:25 NKJV

Father, around the office I see people carrying self-help books to read during their lunch breaks. Each month another title makes the best-seller list. Yet, few have enough substance to be enduring classics.

Lord, when I study my human nature, I find many constants in my character—I am sinful, selfish, full of pride, sometimes afraid, and always facing death. The Bible addresses all these issues. Your Word is more thorough than any contemporary book that would try to show me how to improve myself without Your assistance. May I always remember to turn to Your enduring guidebook for daily living and eternal salvation.

Day 273
Helping Hands

*If any man or woman that believeth have
widows, let them relieve them, and let not
the church be charged; that it may relieve
them that are widows indeed.*

1 TIMOTHY 5:16

As my parents age and need more and more help
from me, remind me that other help is available,
Father. Part-time companions or nursing aides
can ease my family's time burdens and make it
possible for my parents to stay at home. Senior
citizen centers can provide quality activities and
care for the elderly. Meals-on-Wheels or other
similar programs can assure proper nutrition
for those still living on their own. The costs are
minimal and often absorbed by insurance. My
family and I will provide all we can, but there is
no shame in asking for help when it is needed.
You have provided these helpers for us; let us
use them wisely, Lord.

Day 274
Accepting Correction

Behold, happy is the man whom God correcteth:
therefore despise not thou the chastening of the
Almighty: for he maketh sore, and bindeth up:
he woundeth, and his hands make whole.
JOB 5:17–18

When You must correct me, Father, it does not immediately make me happy. It sometimes makes me struggle to get loose and go my own way, especially when I don't recognize that I am dealing with Your correction. It's easier to blame someone else. But eventually I see a pattern or You open my eyes in other ways, and I stop running away from You because I know that You not only correct but also heal. Your correction lasts only a moment; its blessings are eternal. When I realize You are so concerned for me and want to help me, I am filled with gratitude and willing to be led in the right direction.

Day 275
Not Wavering

But let him ask in faith, nothing wavering.
For he that wavereth is like a wave of the
sea driven with the wind and tossed.
JAMES 1:6

I've been in rough seas, Lord. I know what it is like to be at the mercy of the waves, and I do not like it. If my whole life were similar to the experience of being driven by the wind, I would not only be miserable, I would never get anywhere. To me, faith is a very big ship with big motors and a captain who knows what He's doing. Faith keeps me on course. Sometimes I waver. I don't like the looks of the waves ahead; I fear we may be going in the wrong direction. But I have a captain who never makes an error, and the ship He commands is big and strong enough for any wave.

Day 276
Working for God's Glory

*Every man's work shall be made
manifest. . .the fire shall try every
man's work of what sort it is.*
1 CORINTHIANS 3:13

In the end, Father, You will be the judge of my
lifetime of work; and I know You don't care if I
work behind a cash register or an oak desk with
a five-line telephone. It's not what I do that matters, but how I do it. Am I a cheerful worker?
Am I an honest worker? Am I a worker whose
love for You is evident in what I say and how I
treat my fellow workers? Do I care more for my
brothers and sisters than for my next paycheck?
I am Your ambassador, Lord; and every day I try
to show Your love to those who do not know You.
I pray that when the time comes, You will find
me worthy.

Day 277
Jesus' Compassion

*Jesus answered and said unto her,
Martha, Martha, thou art careful
and troubled about many things.*
LUKE 10:41

You showed so much compassion when Martha asked You to send Mary back to her work, Lord. You understood that she was worried about the many details involved in entertaining. Your words demonstrated how much You cared for her and acknowledged that You knew how much she was caught up in providing You a good meal, not something just thrown together. That dinner was the way Martha chose to show her love for You.

Sometimes a kind word of understanding is all I need when I feel overwhelmed, Lord. The circumstances may not change, but I feel better about my burdens when someone simply acknowledges them. Let me give the same compassion to those who work so hard for my benefit.

Day 278
"Ye Are Washed"

But ye are washed, but ye are sanctified,
but ye are justified in the name of the
Lord Jesus, and by the Spirit of our God.
1 CORINTHIANS 6:11

On my own, I am totally unworthy of salvation; and nothing I do or say can change that fact, no matter how much I try. I was a sinner; I am a sinner; I will always be a sinner. Yet, despite my disobedience and stubbornness, You value me, Lord. You believe I am worth saving and will go to any length—even to death on a cross—to show me Your everlasting love, for You died for me. You wash away my sins. You make me holy. You stand before the throne of Your Father and claim me as Your own, exempt from sin and judgment. Because of Your sacrifice, I am made worthy. Thank You, my Savior.

Day 279
Salvation

*So Christ was once offered to bear the
sins of many; and unto them that look
for him shall he appear the second
time without sin unto salvation.*
HEBREWS 9:28

How expectantly I wait for You, Jesus. I long to
shed the sin that still hangs on to my soul as I
wait here on earth. Though I know Your salvation is working in my life, my own sin seeks to
control me.

What freedom from sin You have already
given me—but how much more sin needs to be
removed from me! As I trust in You, I know You
are faithful to cleanse my life more each day.

I trust in Your promise and look for the day
when You return, Jesus. I long to be with You.

Day 280
The Fruitful Congregation

*The harvest truly is great, but the labourers
are few: pray ye therefore the Lord of
the harvest, that he would send forth
labourers into his harvest.*

LUKE 10:2

No fruitful congregation can be the result of one person's work, no matter how dedicated that person may be. Every leader must have followers, or who is there to be led? I thank You for all those in the church who spend their time and energy doing Your work. Remind them that their contributions are both needed and appreciated, especially when I begin to take their work for granted.

At the same time, show me if I am holding back from personally playing a part in Your harvest. My time and talents may seem limited, but You know how to use me, if only I am open to Your calling. I want our congregation to be fruitful.

Day 281
Unearned Grace

And I will have mercy upon her that had not obtained mercy; and I will say to them which were not my people, Thou art my people; and they shall say, Thou art my God.
HOSEA 2:23

O Lord, how great is Your mercy to me. You owed me nothing because I paid You no heed, yet You called me. When I walked far from You, You called me to turn to Your path.

Thank You for caring for me when I wallowed in sin. I did nothing to earn Your grace, yet You gave it to me anyway. May Your great mercy be reflected in my life as I pass on mercy to those who sin against me. May mercy flow freely in my life.

Day 282
God's Faithfulness

*And thine age shall be clearer than
the noonday: thou shalt shine forth,
thou shalt be as the morning.*

JOB 11:17

Thank You, Lord, for Your promise to make me shine, even in my last years. Physically, I may not always feel perfect, but I can still glow for You with a peaceful and trusting spirit. Even when my body does not work perfectly, I can still pray for others. My work for Your kingdom may be just starting.

Keep me trusting in You, Father, aware that You have not left me by the side of the road. I want to reflect Your love and faithfulness every moment of my life.

Day 283
Fearproof

And fear not them which kill the body,
but are not able to kill the soul.
MATTHEW 10:28

How wonderful, Father God, to know that even my most feared enemy does not have final control over me. Even if he put me to death, he could not part my soul from Your love.

I'm not facing death today, but I face fears that feel like death. That killjoy Satan tells me that by following You, I kill off every chance to fulfill certain hopes and dreams. A thousand small deaths attack my soul.

Keep me obedient to Your love; help me trust that You will bring me good things. I need faith to see blessings instead of fears.

Day 284
Wrong Ideas

*As the Scriptures say, "I will destroy the
wisdom of the wise and discard the
intelligence of the intelligent."*
1 CORINTHIANS 1:19 NLT

You know how much we treasure our ideas, Lord.
The things we think—the beliefs we hold—are
precious to us. But You promise us that human
ideas are limited, and even our most brilliant
ones pale compared to Your power.

When other people's bright ideas would
hurt me, I'm glad You're still in control. It's comforting to know that nothing gets past You or is
beyond Your control. But help me to remember
that Your power also limits my human wisdom.
When I think I'm being the smartest, my idea
could be valueless if it doesn't side with Your
wisdom.

Keep me in Your wise ways, Lord. I don't
want my best ideas discarded because they
were dead wrong.

Day 285
Compassion and Justice

"The LORD, the LORD, the compassionate and gracious God, slow to anger, abounding in love and faithfulness, maintaining love to thousands, and forgiving wickedness, rebellion and sin. Yet he does not leave the guilty unpunished."
EXODUS 34:6–7 NIV

How faithful You are to me, Lord, and to everyone else who trusts in You. Over and over I've seen You work mercifully in the lives of my Christian friends and fellow churchgoers. I see it in the lives of believers who share their faith publicly and in my own life too. You never let us down, Lord, even when we go through trouble. You're patient and loving, forgiving our sins.

But You're also just and don't let the guilty—even Christians—get away with wrongdoing. Your justice is as perfect as Your love, Jesus. Thank You for that perfect balance.

Day 286
God's Rescue

*My eyes are always on the LORD, for he
rescues me from the traps of my enemies.
Turn to me and have mercy, for I am
alone and in deep distress.*
PSALM 25:15–16 NLT

When I'm hurting, I'm glad others try to ease
my pain. But often they provide only limited answers or solutions to my grief. No matter who
else stands by me, when I'm lonely and aching,
Lord, I need Your all-powerful healing touch.
Only You can reach the agonizing places that no
one else can get to. Though people do their best
to give me good advice or comfort, only Your
Spirit touches my innermost spots.

Others try to rescue me, but only You can
take complete charge of the situation and bring
relief. I need Your hand on my life when I feel
lonely and afflicted. Thank You for Your aid,
Lord.

Day 287
Respect for Others

*"Watch out! Be on your guard against
all kinds of greed; life does not consist
in an abundance of possessions."*
LUKE 12:15 NIV

Though the world values me according to what I own or how much I make in a year, I'm glad You don't, Lord. There is so much more to life than money and things. But I've noticed that even though I like being judged by better means, I often give a wealthy person more respect than the poor but faithful person. Forgive me, Lord, for judging wrongly in such an important matter.

I want to value people as You do—so help me to view them through Your lens, not the world's. When I do that, I will befriend those who are important to You, even if they don't have a dime in their pockets.

Day 288
God Cares

*Behold, the Lord's hand is not
shortened, that it cannot save;
nor His ear heavy, that it cannot hear.*
ISAIAH 59:1 NKJV

It warms my heart to know that You are not ignoring me, even when I can't feel Your touch, Lord. If troubles face me and I'm tempted to think You don't care, You've promised me that isn't so. You're still working in my life, even if I can't sense it.

When You don't rush to my aid, You ask me to continue trusting in You. It's not time to give up. Though help isn't here yet, I can count on its being on the way.

I'm glad You hear my prayers and save me. If I have faith, Your hand will reach out to me at just the right moment. Thank You, Jesus, that Your salvation may be only a moment away.

Day 289
Walking with God

Noah was a just man and perfect in his generations, and Noah walked with God.
GENESIS 6:9

Lord, I am defined by whom I choose as my heroes and after whom I pattern my life. Others interpret my character by those with whom I walk. I want to be like the heroes of old, those people of renown in the Old Testament, who were described as having "walked with God."

Dear Father, give me the determination to walk at Your side. I seek an honorable walk that shows Your power and character. I know that I am not walking alone; You are with me. I have victory over impossible circumstances because I have placed myself in Your footsteps.

Day 290
Vital Giving

*The thoughts of the diligent tend
only to plenteousness; but of every
one that is hasty only to want.*

PROVERBS 21:5

Lord, it seems every cause has a compelling reason for me to support its effort. I find it difficult to separate the vital few from the trivial many. I cannot learn enough about every group's programs to fully support what they are doing. Give me the wisdom to direct my support to those who are carrying out Your will. I pray I will always be willing to make sacrifices, but keep me from being a wasteful giver.

Heavenly Father, guide me to practical ways that I can support those who are doing Your will.

Day 291
For Unity of Believers

*And the glory which thou gavest
me I have given them; that they
may be one, even as we are one.*

JOHN 17:22

Righteous Father, I am humbled when I realize
that Jesus, on the night He was betrayed, prayed
for the unity of believers. I look at Your Word
through different eyes than other Christians
and often cannot fully agree with them. Help me
focus on our many vital common beliefs rather
than our few trivial differences. Help me see the
strength in unity and the danger of discord.

Often it is easy to agree if the agreement is to
do nothing. Let my agreement be to act and do,
not sit back and wait. Let me join the fellowship
of believers so we become a force for righteousness, just as Jesus prayed for.

Day 292
Pardon

And I will cleanse them from all their iniquity, whereby they have sinned against me; and I will pardon all their iniquities, whereby they have sinned, and whereby they have transgressed against me.

JEREMIAH 33:8

Father, there was a time when I had the nagging uncertainty about whether I had been truly forgiven. I had remorse for my sins, I repented of my actions, and I desired to understand the truth of the Gospel. But as a new Christian, I tried unsuccessfully to live up to the contradictory advice I was given.

Today I know that I cannot earn a place in Your kingdom by what I do or do not do. Instead, I bring You a heart of obedience and an affection for spiritual matters. I am secure in the knowledge of Your saving grace. I honor You with a heart of obedience and know that when I fail, You will pardon me.

Day 293
Recreational Slander

For I have heard the slander of many.
PSALM 31:13

We are surrounded by lies and slander. Politicians twist the facts to prove whatever they want to prove. Corporate leaders play with the numbers until they come out the "right" way. But it's not only the powerful who slander—I can get an earful of it at any community meeting or market. Some of this is recreational slander, passing on to others the little lies I have just heard. I tell myself that gossip is harmless, at least until I am its victim and experience its pain. Father, there is no way I can avoid hearing gossip and slander, but I don't have to delight in it, let alone spread it. When I hear something I know another would love to hear, make me stop and think before I speak. What is to be gained by spreading the news?

Day 294
Fear Not

*God is our refuge and strength, a very
present help in trouble. Therefore will
not we fear, though the earth be removed,
and though the mountains be carried
into the midst of the sea.*
PSALM 46:1–2

When troubles come, I never have to face them
alone. Thank You, Lord, for always being with
me as my refuge and strength. Friends can fail,
families can split apart, my whole world can be
shaken to its foundation, leaving me dazed and
disoriented, but You never change. Your truths
are forever. You do not shrug off my concerns
and move on. You are "a very present help in
trouble," standing firmly at my side whatever
happens, guiding my actions, and giving me the
strength to carry on. When all else fails, when
friends and family desert me, I put my trust in
You and am never disappointed.

Day 295
Knowledge and Understanding

For the LORD giveth wisdom: out of his mouth cometh knowledge and understanding. He layeth up sound wisdom for the righteous.

PROVERBS 2:6–7

I know that wisdom is more than knowledge, Father. Knowledge is helpful in life; and I encourage my children to seek it because it is beneficial to know history, languages, science, and mathematics. But even the uneducated may have wisdom, which is understanding how to apply knowledge in our daily lives. The most learned of people can still embrace evil, but the wise know better. You promise to lay up sound wisdom for the righteous so they will understand how You want them to live and thereby bring glory to Your name. If I have to choose between giving my children knowledge or wisdom, I would choose to give them an understanding of the wisdom that comes from You.

Day 296
Fear versus Faith

And he said unto them, Why are ye so
fearful? how is it that ye have no faith?
MARK 4:40

Lord Jesus, today I feel as if You are asleep while
I'm all alone at the tiller of my life. Waves rise up
around me, and You seem not to see them. The
boat of my life rocks, and You don't grab the tiller
from my hand. Fear fills my soul.

I know, Lord, that as a Christian I need not
fear the waves. Doubt disrupted my vision and
made me grab the tiller in the first place. Return
my eyes to their proper focus: You.

Day 297
Blessings of Mercy

He that despiseth his neighbour
sinneth: but he that hath mercy
on the poor, happy is he.
PROVERBS 14:21

Forgive me, Lord, for looking down on those who lack money, possessions, or knowledge of You. I'm sometimes tempted to think I'm better than they are, though Your Word clearly states that's not true.

Help me to heed Your warning and eagerly share what You've given me with those in need. Remind me that I count on Your mercy in my life as much as they count on it in theirs.

Even when sin filled every corner of my life, You did not despise me. Your mercy turned me into a new person. May I share that blessing with those whose spirits or pocketbooks are needy.

Day 298
Christian Fearlessness

So we say with confidence, "The Lord
is my helper; I will not be afraid.
What can mere mortals do to me?"
HEBREWS 13:6 NIV

When my enemies stand before me, Lord, fear is the first emotion that covers me. Uncertain about the future, I begin to worry about the things I could lose to these people.

Your promise tells me I have nothing to fear. What can I lose that is not already in Your hand? What can I lose that is not already in Your control? With Your help, I am secure and guarded against every attack.

Thank You for Your protection. Keep me from fear and strengthen my trust in You.

Day 299
Endurance

But he that shall endure unto the end,
the same shall be saved.
MATTHEW 24:13

Lord, I must admit that words like *patience* and *endurance* aren't my favorites. They make me think of gritting my teeth and bearing up under troubles—and I never look forward to troubles.

Give me Your vision of patience and endurance, Jesus. You came to earth and bore my sins, when heaven was Your rightful home. You endured much on earth so that I could relate to You. Help me see the value in patiently enduring hardship. I look forward with joy to eternity with You. Strengthen me, Lord, to be patient until that day.

Day 300
Healing Love

I will heal their backsliding, I will
love them freely: for mine anger
is turned away from him.
HOSEA 14:4

Even though I've slid away from faith, thank You, Lord, that I can hang on to this promise, which says You still love me. All I need to do is turn to You again for forgiveness.

Forgive me, God, for my double-mindedness. Part of me wants to believe You, but fear and doubt have drawn me away from Your love. I don't want doubt to destroy my love for You. Heal me from the things that would separate us.

Yours is a wonderful love that does not count wrongs. Help me live in that love every day.

Day 301
Worry for Tomorrow

"Therefore do not worry about tomorrow,
for tomorrow will worry about itself.
Each day has enough trouble of its own."
MATTHEW 6:34 NIV

Some days have plenty of trouble, Lord, and it's easy for me to look ahead and wonder what the next day will bring. Then I start thinking about a week, a month, or a year ahead, and soon my whole life looks bleak. Once I start worrying, it's hard to stop.

Help me to remember that all You've given me is today—a single twenty-four-hour period to deal with. I need to focus on what I have before me in this day, not those that lie beyond. And for this day, I can ask for—and receive—all the help I need from You.

Help me, Jesus, with today's worries. Then tomorrow may not be a concern after all.

Day 302
Forgiveness

"The Lord is slow to anger, abounding in love and forgiving sin and rebellion."
Numbers 14:18 niv

When I've done wrong, Lord, I'm so glad You've promised to be slow to anger and quick to forgive. Thank You for not taking out Your anger on me.

But when I have to forgive someone else, I really appreciate what it took for You to forgive me. I begin to doubt I can pardon the one who's caused that hurt. On my own, I could never express Your forgiveness because it just isn't in my dark heart. Thank You for giving me a new heart—one reflecting Yours—that responds with forgiveness as Your Spirit infiltrates every corner.

To be like You, I need Your Spirit's filling. Come into my spirit today, and erase the anger that gets in the way of my being just like You.

Day 303
Sharing

And God will generously provide all you need.
Then you will always have everything you need
and plenty left over to share with others.
2 Corinthians 9:8 nlt

Lord, You've given me so much. Thank You for the generous way You've cared for all my needs. Though I may not always have a lot of extra money in the bank, my true necessities are always covered. And I'm continually rich in Your blessings.

Whatever I do have, Lord, help me share abundantly with others. I know that when I give out of what You've blessed me with, You always replenish my store. Whether my need is cash, food, or a place to live, I can trust in Your faithfulness every day.

Thank You for being ever faithful, Father. Your generosity blesses my life.

Day 304
God's Redeeming Love

*[God] redeems your life from the pit
and crowns you with love and compassion.*
PSALM 103:4 NIV

Bound by sin, my life was worthy of a pit, Lord. But You came and redeemed me. The transformation Your love made in me can hardly be explained.

Thank You for buying me back from sin before I was even born. Two thousand years ago, when Your Son died on the cross for my sins, You made the transaction. But those years between have no influence as Your redemption powerfully impacts my life.

Not only have You saved me, Lord, You've crowned my life with love and compassion. As You have blessed my life so incredibly, help me use those blessings to reach out to all who need Your redeeming love.

Day 305
Generosity

A generous person will prosper; whoever refreshes others will be refreshed.
PROVERBS 11:25 NIV

I want to be generous, Lord, because that's what You are. From the moment I accepted Your Son, I took part in Your spiritual blessings, experiencing freedom from sin. But You've also given me physical and intellectual blessings I can share with others. I cannot rightly withhold anything You ask me to use to help another.

As I give to others, You promise to refresh me. Sometimes You revive me spiritually instead of returning a physical blessing, but You always give generously, beyond what I expected.

Thank You for giving me so much, Lord. Help me not to hoard but to share Your prosperity.

Day 306
Grace

Wherefore we receiving a kingdom which cannot be moved, let us have grace, whereby we may serve God acceptably with reverence and godly fear.
HEBREWS 12:28

Father, I know that I cannot obtain absolute perfection in my life. I appeal to You for Your mercy. I know that Your forgiveness is without limit, provided I exercise the same forgiveness with others. I pray for the help of the Holy Spirit so I can forgive repeatedly without harboring resentment.

Thank You for Your generous grace. I ask that Your mercy flow over me. I pray that You will favor my undertakings and wrap them in Your clemency so that even when I fail, I will be under Your protection.

Day 307
A Personal Prayer

And this is life eternal, that they
might know thee the only true God,
and Jesus Christ, whom thou hast sent.
JOHN 17:3

Heavenly Father, in this prayer I want to speak to You about myself. I pray that it is not a selfish prayer, for my ultimate goal is to be right with You. Please make a way for me to avoid sin and help me to accept Your forgiveness when I do sin. I long to be right with You. Direct my steps to always be in the path of righteousness.

Father, help me recognize the work You have given me to do, and assist me as I try to glorify You. Stamp Your name on my heart so that I may live eternally in Your presence.

Day 308
Giving of Myself

And whosoever will be chief among you,
let him be your servant: Even as the Son of
man came not to be ministered unto, but to
minister, and to give his life a ransom for many.
MATTHEW 20:27–28

As I contemplate all the activities that demand my attention, I think of You, Jesus. You did the work of a servant by washing the feet of the apostles. Please help me remember that the greatest in the kingdom of heaven is not the one being served, but the humble one doing the serving.

Sometimes I find it easier to give from a distance than to become personally involved in situations. Help me, Lord, to fulfill the mission to serve others. I need Your strength to meet my obligations to my family, my coworkers, and members of my community.

Day 309
Trust in His Defense

But let all those that put their trust in thee rejoice: let them ever shout for joy, because thou defendest them: let them also that love thy name be joyful in thee.
PSALM 5:11

Thankfully, dear Jesus, I have never been falsely accused of a crime and had to stand trial. Should that unfortunate event occur, I would want a skilled defense attorney to plead my case and believable witnesses to establish my innocence.

Lord, the Bible says that You defend those who believe in You. When Satan brings charges against my life or character, I am encouraged that You are my defense attorney and also my witness. Thank You for accepting my faith and trust as the evidence You need to render the verdict, "Not guilty! Case closed!"

Day 310
The Seller of Purple

And a certain woman named Lydia, a seller of purple. . .which worshipped God, heard us: whose heart the Lord opened, that she attended unto the things which were spoken of Paul.

ACTS 16:14

Lydia had never heard the story of Jesus, even though she worshiped You, Father. She was a businesswoman selling expensive purple cloth she made—a very busy woman. She may just have been curious at first, always interested in new developments; but You opened her heart, and she listened carefully to everything Paul said that day.

I admit that sometimes I don't really listen, Lord. I have too much to think of and too little time to absorb every sermon the way I should. But You promise You will come into my heart and live there if I welcome You, just as You did for Lydia. Come into my heart, Lord Jesus.

Day 311
Household Peacekeeping

A soft answer turneth away wrath:
but grievous words stir up anger.
PROVERBS 15:1

Most often I am the one who plays the role of
household peacekeeper, Lord. This is a double-
edged duty. Not only must I pacify the children
and my spouse on their bad days, I must also
see that I don't contribute to the mayhem
through venting my own anger. When we're
having a "she hit me first" day, Lord, help me
hold my tongue until I can reply with a healing answer, not an angry one. Give me calming
words, not words that will hurt or cause even
more upset. And when I am angry myself, let me
be an example of how to deal effectively with
anger. Help me be the peacekeeper, never the
one who stirs up more anger.

Day 312
Evidence

Now faith is the substance of things hoped for,
the evidence of things not seen.
HEBREWS 11:1

Lord, astronomers have recently discovered distant moons and planets they cannot see through even the strongest of telescopes. By observing the effects these bodies have on other bodies— changes in orbit, for example—they know these distant bodies simply must be there, or their effects would not be there. This is "evidence of things not seen," perhaps even the "substance of things hoped for." I admit I do not totally understand how the astronomers do this, but I find it comforting.

There is so much I do not understand about You. Still, I can see the effects of Your actions, the evidence that You are still active in my daily life and the lives of others. I do not need to physically see You to believe. Your evidence is everywhere.

Day 313
Living by Faith

And the life which I now live in the flesh
I live by the faith of the Son of God,
who loved me, and gave himself for me.
GALATIANS 2:20

Lord, You know I am a miserable sinner unworthy of Your blessings, let alone Your salvation. On my own, I am a hopeless case. I gleefully jump over one sin and land right in another. Yet You love me, You came to earth to save me, and You entreat Your Father to forgive my sins and accept me as a beloved child. While my faith is small and puny, Yours is perfect and mighty. The life I am living right now is not the result of my faith in You but of Your faith in me. Thank You for Your sacrifice that saves me and makes me whole. Without Your perfect faith, I would be doomed.

Day 314
Family Justice

But why dost thou judge thy brother? or why dost thou set at nought thy brother? for we shall all stand before the judgment seat of Christ.

ROMANS 14:10

I understand that it is not my job to judge my sister or brother, Lord. When we were young, that was the duty of our parents, and they did a fair job of it with only a few bad verdicts. My brothers and sisters through blood deserve the same patience and love as those in my Christian family. If I can forgive a nonrelative who hurts me, I can be even more forgiving within my family. If I can give charity to strangers, I need to be at least as generous to those related to me. Give me Your guidance, Lord. Reveal the needs of my brothers and sisters—whether they are physical, emotional, or spiritual—and incline my heart to them.

Day 315
The Evil One

Neither death, nor life, nor angels, nor principalities, nor powers, nor things present, nor things to come, nor height, nor depth, nor any other creature, shall be able to separate us from the love of God, which is in Christ Jesus our Lord.
ROMANS 8:38–39

I know the evil one's main goal is to separate me from You, Father, by any means possible; and there are lots of possible means he can use. I have much to fear from him because I am weak, and my faith is imperfect. But this is one battle he can never win. He can never stop You from loving me. You sent Your Son to save me and make me whole, and the devil will not prevail. I am Your adopted child through Christ. I am Your beloved child. Thank You, Father.

Day 316
God's Joy

Yet I will rejoice in the LORD,
I will joy in the God of my salvation.
HABAKKUK 3:18

Even when life is miserable, I can rejoice in You, Lord. Pressures on the job and financial troubles can't stop that joy. Nothing disrupts Your plan of salvation for me or the change You've made in my heart.

Thank You, Lord, for lifting my heart in joy when I think of Your salvation. When the world seems empty or threatening, I can still rejoice. On even the worst day, I can feel joy that You separated me from my sins and will never count them against me. Thank You, Lord.

Day 317
The Spirit of Adoption

For ye have not received the spirit of bondage again to fear; but ye have received the Spirit of adoption, whereby we cry, Abba, Father.

ROMANS 8:15

Little children have many fears, some of which they cannot explain even to their parents. They run to their parents' room at night, cold and shaking in terror, and beg to be allowed into the big, safe bed. They know their parents will protect them from whatever fills their nightmares.

In the dark of the night, I sometimes find myself in the clutch of fear too. Because I am Your adopted child through Christ, I know You love me, and I cry out to You. Through Your Spirit, You calm and protect me as I cry, "Abba, Father."

Day 318
My Unbelief

If we believe not, yet he abideth faithful: he cannot deny himself.
2 TIMOTHY 2:13

Thank You, Lord, that my faithfulness does not depend on my abilities. I try with all my might to be faithful, yet I can still end up in an awful mess. The good things I start often end up wrong. I hold fast to things I should let go of and avoid things that would help Your kingdom grow.

I praise You for the faithfulness that is part of Your perfect nature. It never changes or leaves me helpless. Thank You for that faithfulness, Lord. May it seep into my heart and soul as I follow You today.

Day 319
Love's Courage

O love the LORD, all ye his saints: for the LORD preserveth the faithful, and plentifully rewardeth the proud doer. Be of good courage, and he shall strengthen your heart, all ye that hope in the LORD.
PSALM 31:23–24

When my courage seems so small and slips away, when sin seeks to pull me from Your path, Lord, remind me of these verses. I need only trust in You, the One who keeps me safe and brings good things into my life. You reward my feeble efforts and multiply them through Your strength as I simply love You and respond to You in faith.

I want to be strong—in You and for You. Give me courage each day. When evil seems to abound and sin distracts me from Your way, thank You that Your love abounds still more.

Day 320
Living by Faith

*But that no one is justified by the
law in the sight of God is evident,
for "the just shall live by faith."*
GALATIANS 3:11 NKJV

I can't imagine keeping Your law perfectly, Lord.
But even if I could, it would not do me the ultimate good: it would not gain me heaven. How
thankful I am that You don't require perfect
obedience—just faith.

But I can't even live by faith under my own
steam. Temptations come, and I quickly give in,
despite my love for You. Only Your Spirit makes
the heart change that keeps me faithful to You in
thought and deed. Fill my heart with Your Spirit,
Lord. Make me true to You, despite the temptations. I want to live in faith, not doubt or fear.

Day 321
End of the Curse

*No longer will there be a curse upon anything.
For the throne of God and of the Lamb will be
there, and his servants will worship him.*
REVELATION 22:3 NLT

What a glorious time this will be, Lord, when sin
no longer rules the world. In Your eternal kingdom, all those who believe will do nothing but
worship You. Satan will no longer trap us, and
our minds and spirits will totally focus on You.

I can't quite imagine what heaven will be
like, Lord; but I look forward to a time without
sin, when I can draw close to You in a new way
and serve You perfectly. When life becomes hard,
I focus on this promise. I long to be with You for
eternity, Jesus.

Thank You for this eternal promise.

Day 322
Faith in Jesus

*"Blessed is anyone who does not
stumble on account of me."*
LUKE 7:23 NIV

Some things You said, Jesus, present even believers with a challenge. I have to admit that You didn't make the Christian faith too easy. Sometimes I'm not comfortable with Your "hard sayings" because I don't understand them—or I don't like what they tell me to do.

But if I trust in You in spite of my lack of comfort or understanding, You promise I will be blessed. In my Christian walk, I've already seen that obedience gets me farther than qualms. Challenging doubt with faith brings a blessing, while settling for doubt just causes trouble. Help me stand up to doubts instead of giving in to them.

Thank You for that blessing, Lord. Keep me trusting in You.

Day 323
Generosity

Remember this: Whoever sows sparingly will also reap sparingly, and whoever sows generously will also reap generously.

2 Corinthians 9:6 niv

This verse reminds me that You give generously, Lord, and expect me to follow in Your footsteps. Because You've bestowed so much on me, I can share Your generosity. How will others know what You're really like if I hoard my experience with You, the gifts You've given me, and even the physical blessings You've allowed me to have?

Open my spirit to Your will, Lord, and help me give from a generous heart so I can experience Your joy in generosity. When I reach heaven, instead of a poor harvest that resulted from today's greed, I'd like to see a full field of good plants that took root in Your kingdom.

Day 324
Persistence

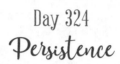

"But you, be strong and do not let your hands be weak, for your work shall be rewarded!"
2 CHRONICLES 15:7 NKJV

Lord, though You gave this promise to King Asa, I know it's also true for me. When I work hard, You can bless me in many ways.

Right now, as I seek work, help me do so consistently, as if I were working for You, not just myself. When I send out many resumes and get few responses, keep me going even when discouragement tempts me to quit.

If I keep my hands strong, typing at the computer or filling out applications for work, I know You will be faithful. Eventually I'll find the job You had in mind for me all along.

Day 325
A Tool for Every Task

I therefore, the prisoner of the Lord,
beseech you that ye walk worthy
of the vocation wherewith ye are called.
EPHESIANS 4:1

Father, I am impressed when I watch a skilled carpenter or auto mechanic at work. I am struck by how they select a tool that is perfectly fitted for the task at hand.

Dear Lord, I see that You have given me particular skills and abilities. Others can fill in for me when I do not do the jobs for which I have been created. However, You have called me into service to apply my unique talents to those tasks that I do best. May I never evade my responsibilities by claiming that someone else is better qualified.

Day 326
The KISS Principle

But I fear, lest by any means, as the serpent beguiled Eve through his subtilty, so your minds should be corrupted from the simplicity that is in Christ.

2 CORINTHIANS 11:3

Lord, the management principle known as KISS—"Keep It Simple, Stupid"—does have its merits (despite the "Stupid" reference). I am involved in far too many organizations and activities that litter my mind and fritter away my time.

Father, I long for simplicity in my relationship with You. Please help me manage my time so I can focus on a better kinship with You. Release me from the clutter of unimportant activities that infringe on my time and attention. I pray that I will set aside quiet time for reflection and communication with You.

Day 327
Synergy

Be of the same mind one toward another.
Mind not high things, but condescend to men of
low estate. Be not wise in your own conceits.
ROMANS 12:16

Lord, wonderful moments occur when I work so well with another person that we seem to act as one individual. Our ideas function perfectly together, and our progress toward our goal goes more quickly than our individual efforts would. We have a shared objective, and we use our different talents to accomplish our unified purpose.

Father, please help me recognize that differences between people are not negative but positive. Give me the insight to see how I can harmonize with them to make a pleasing whole. Guide me to be a cooperative individual as I work within Your kingdom.

Day 328
Victory

Therefore, my beloved brethren, be ye stedfast, unmoveable, always abounding in the work of the Lord, forasmuch as ye know that your labour is not in vain in the Lord.

1 CORINTHIANS 15:58

In my daily work, I rarely experience victory. I clean up one mess and move on to the next, knowing even greater messes are just around the corner. I never really seem to get anywhere, to win any battles, or see anything truly completed. There are precious few victories in my work. But You encourage me to hang in there and keep on working for You, because You have already won the victory in the most important battle of all—the battle for my soul. My daily problems come and go, yet if I remain steadfast and dedicated, doing the work You have given me to do, I am confident that my reward awaits me. Thank You, Lord.

Day 329
Unrewarded Kindness

*Inasmuch as ye have done it unto
one of the least of these my brethren,
ye have done it unto me.*
MATTHEW 25:40

There's a popular saying today that "No good deed goes unpunished." Sometimes it feels that way. But no one promised that hospitality and brotherly love would be easy. Certainly there is no guarantee that it will be rewarded here on earth. I just have to continue to treat people with dignity and hope I don't get emotionally mugged in return. Yet You have promised that my good deeds will someday be rewarded, and I trust Your Word. When my cynical attitude keeps me from performing acts of hospitality, give me the faith and strength to do what needs to be done, not because I want a reward but because it is an honor to do Your work.

Day 330
The Lonely Sparrow

*I watch, and am as a sparrow
alone upon the house top.*
PSALM 102:7

Some days I feel just like that lonely sparrow, Lord. Everyone else is crowded around the bird feeder, caring for their babies or flitting to and fro on urgent business; but I sit alone, just watching. What am I looking for? Will I ever find a flock of my own to join? Will anyone ever fly up and join me on the housetop, easing this sense of separation I feel so acutely? Yet You tell me that not one sparrow falls without Your noticing and that I am of more value than many sparrows (Matthew 10:29, 31). You see me there alone on my rooftop, Lord. You feel my loneliness, and suddenly I belong—and I can sing a song of joy.

Day 331
Joy in Uncertainty

*Thou hast put gladness in my heart,
more than in the time that their corn
and their wine increased.*

PSALM 4:7

Thank You, Lord, for allowing me to celebrate, even when life is uncertain. When I trust in Your salvation, I don't have to depend on circumstances for joy. As I follow Your way and receive the blessings of Your righteousness, my heart fills with joy.

Though I may not know the outcome of everything in my life, I am trusting in You, and I know You care for all my needs. How my heart rejoices that I can trust in You!

Thank You that I can celebrate Your love and holiness each day. May that celebration be sweeter because I have put my trust in You.

Day 332
God's Glory

*If ye be reproached for the name of Christ,
happy are ye; for the spirit of glory and of
God resteth upon you: on their part he is evil
spoken of, but on your part he is glorified.*
1 PETER 4:14

When others speak ill of me because I tell them
of Your love, I glorify You, Lord. What an amazing
promise! To be glorified for my stand for You
is a blessing.

But I must admit, I don't often think of it as
a blessing. I'm more likely to agree with people
than take a firm stand against them. It's not
pleasant being criticized and condemned.

Remind me, Father, that no one on earth
gives the final condemnation. Though people
may heap harsh words or actions on me, they
only have temporal power. Yours is the final
opinion—the one that really counts.

Day 333
Mount Zion

*They that trust in the LORD shall be as mount
Zion, which cannot be removed, but abideth
for ever. As the mountains are round about
Jerusalem, so the LORD is round about his
people from henceforth even for ever.*
PSALM 125:1–2

I come to You seeking a safe haven, Father, a
town nestled in a mountain chain, safe from any
attack from the outside world. I come seeking
peace and the freedom to follow Your way. Of
course I know there is no such place, geograph-
ically speaking; Jerusalem fell often, mountains
or not.

What I seek is Your presence, Father. I trust
in You, and You have promised to be with me
forever, surrounding me with Your sheltering
arms. I seek to be like Your mountain—faithful
forever, secure in Your love, unmovable in times
of peril.

Day 334
The Crown of Life

Blessed is the man that endureth temptation:
for when he is tried, he shall receive the
crown of life, which the Lord hath
promised to them that love him.
JAMES 1:12

Lord, I am on the lookout for the big temptations of the Ten Commandments, and by and large I can avoid them because they are so obvious. It's the little pebbles on the road of life that worry me, that make me stumble and fear for my life with You.

You came to save me, to throw my sin to the bottom of the seas, to make me pure enough to receive the crown of life and be with You for eternity. My duty is to love You; my sins I leave for You to handle because I cannot. I am not afraid.

Day 335
My Blessings

And all these blessings shall come on thee,
and overtake thee, if thou shalt hearken
unto the voice of the LORD thy God.

DEUTERONOMY 28:2

Father, I thank You for Your promises and provision. You touch my life in every way, never denying me that which I truly need, helping me flourish. Without You, I would surely fail; but with You, anything is possible for me.

Day 336
Unfailing Love

Love never fails.
1 CORINTHIANS 13:8 NKJV

I couldn't call my love for others "unfailing," Lord. When people irritate me, it's so easy to make unloving choices. Though I want to draw others to You by my own faithfulness, my own sin gets in the way; and I find myself being a traitor to Your kingdom.

Though my caring ability fails often, I know from experience and Your Word that Yours never does. I'm incredibly glad of this promise because I know how much I need Your love every moment of my life. If You failed to shower me with Your affection, my days would really be a mess.

Fill me with Your unfailing love for both those I relate to easily and those who are a challenge just to be with. Love them through me with Your unending compassion.

Day 337
Cleansed from Sin

*For he who lacks these things is shortsighted,
even to blindness, and has forgotten that
he was cleansed from his old sins.*
2 PETER 1:9 NKJV

I don't want to forget that You completely cleansed me from my old sins, Lord. To do so would be to live in a time when I didn't know You. Your love and forgiveness have changed me and put all that's behind far from me, Lord. No longer do I have to sin because I have no other option. You've put the ability to do good in my heart, and that's the way I want to live each day.

Let me not be shortsighted, ignoring what You've already done for me. Instead give me the twenty-twenty vision of Your kingdom. Then help me use that sight to walk with You.

Day 338
God Hears Prayer

The LORD is far from the wicked,
but he hears the prayer of the righteous.
PROVERBS 15:29 NIV

Amazing, Lord—You hear every request I pray! Even when I don't receive a quick response or when You say "no," You have listened to my supplication. As I ask for the wrong things, You hear that prayer, see to its heart, and work out my problem in a better way that accomplishes Your will. Though I haven't perfectly understood Your ways, You're always open to me.

Because I've accepted Jesus, You've called me righteous and listened to me. But those who don't love Your Son are far from Your ears. They cannot count on answered prayer until they turn to You. Bring them to faith in You, Lord, so You can hear their supplications too.

Day 339
Blessed by God

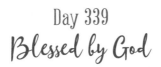

*Only those whose hands and hearts are pure,
who do not worship idols and never tell lies.
They will receive the LORD's blessing and have
right relationship with God their savior.*
PSALM 24:4–5 NLT

This is a tall order, Lord. Who among us has never perpetrated a falsehood on another or lied when confronted with wrongdoing? But that's not the lifestyle You want us to lead; and in Your Spirit, we can have the clean hands and pure heart You require of us.

Cleanse me and fill me with Your Spirit, Lord. Make me entirely clean in You through Your salvation. Then build in me a life that reflects that change. As I put every part of my being in Your hands, I am blessed beyond measure.

Thank You, Lord, for Your new life in my life.

Day 340
Unforgiven Blasphemy

"Assuredly, I say to you, all sins will be forgiven the sons of men, and whatever blasphemies they may utter; but he who blasphemes against the Holy Spirit never has forgiveness, but is subject to eternal condemnation"—because they said, "He has an unclean spirit."

MARK 3:28–30 NKJV

Every sin forgiven! What a wonderful promise, Jesus. Your people rejoice in that truth and see its results in their lives. Each day we bless You for the freedom You have given us.

But anyone who denies that Your message comes from God cannot experience forgiveness; their only "reward" is eternal condemnation. Though those who turn aside from redemption in You should never share Your kingdom, it bothers me that anyone might spend eternity in hell. So I ask You to open those unbelievers' hearts, Lord, to recognize their sin. Please use my testimony to show them the truth.

Day 341
Lighting the Dark

The night is far spent, the day is at hand:
let us therefore cast off the works of darkness,
and let us put on the armour of light.
ROMANS 13:12

Heavenly Father, this valley that I walk in has two different aspects depending on the angle of the sun. In the evening, the shadow of a hill casts the valley into deep gloom. But in the early hours of the day, the valley is bright because it faces the morning sun.

Father, what a difference the sun makes in the natural world, and what a difference when I see my life with the light You provide! When I walk through dark passages in my life, I pray that my eyes will be opened to the illumination You provide. Give me a positive outlook to overcome the dreary times. Keep me in the light of Your blessings.

Day 342
On Autopilot

Learn to do well; seek judgment,
relieve the oppressed, judge the
fatherless, plead for the widow.
ISAIAH 1:17

Lord, I was driving when I realized with a start that I'd passed my turn. I'd taken the same route to work so often that on the weekend, when my destination was in the same direction, I'd continued on as if going to work. I was on autopilot, not thinking of my purpose or where I was going.

Father, in my spiritual life, I sometimes go on autopilot. I unconsciously let religious ceremonies and thoughtless worship substitute for honest and meaningful living. Serving You can cause weariness for me and those around me when it becomes a ritual. Help me develop enthusiasm and delight for a conscious Christian walk.

Day 343
Growing in Forgiveness

For thus saith the LORD of hosts;
after the glory hath he sent me unto the
nations which spoiled you: for he that
toucheth you toucheth the apple of his eye.
ZECHARIAH 2:8

Heavenly Father, I am struck by references in the Old Testament that describe Your people as the apple of Your eye. I realize that I am very precious in Your sight. If I am the apple of Your eye, then I must replicate Your characteristics to be a true offspring of Yours, just as apples reproduce seeds like those from which they originated.

Lord, since I am Your offspring, I need to compare my righteousness to You and not to others. Help me to grow in Your likeness by freely forgiving the offenses of others.

Day 344
Greet Them with a Smile

But straightway Jesus spake unto them, saying,
Be of good cheer; it is I; be not afraid.
MATTHEW 14:27

Dear Jesus, just as You told Your followers to be of good cheer, may I recognize that You want me to heed those words as well. My experience confirms what scientific research has shown— a cheerful personality can overcome physical and mental afflictions. A positive attitude allows the body to heal.

Lord, give me a cheerful disposition, not only to benefit myself but also to bless others. I know that a good attitude can be a great influence for You. Help my joy spread to all those I meet.

Day 345
The Picture Jesus Sees

According as he hath chosen us in him before the foundation of the world, that we should be holy and without blame before him in love.

EPHESIANS 1:4

Dear Lord, with an auto-everything camera, even I can take pictures. But I have found that snapping the shutter does not guarantee a good photo. I've learned to aim the camera to cut out distracting elements such as road signs, to avoid trees growing out of heads, and to keep power lines from cutting across a scenic view. Sometimes I have to use a flash to illuminate a dark subject.

Jesus, in Your honored position of viewing Earth from heaven, what kind of image of my life do You see? Remove all distracting elements from my Christian character. Illuminate me with Your love, and frame me in Your Word. I pray You will compose my life so it presents a pleasing picture to others—and to You.

Day 346
Revive Me

*Nevertheless I have somewhat against
thee, because thou hast left thy first love.
Remember therefore from whence thou art
fallen, and repent, and do the first works.*
REVELATION 2:4–5

Father, I sometimes become so captivated by the
concerns of my daily life that I lose interest in
my spiritual life. I struggle through a morass of
unconcern for others and even for myself. I forget my calling as Your child.

Lord, I acknowledge my apathy and ignorance and realize that my lassitude comes from
a lack of drinking from Your refreshing water. I
need to renew myself with prayer, study of Your
Word, and fellowship with other Christians. Give
me new momentum. Revitalize my life. Restore
the intensity of my first love for You.

Day 347
"Here I Am"

Then shalt thou call, and the
LORD shall answer; thou shalt cry,
and he shall say, Here I am.
ISAIAH 58:9

Father, from my childhood, You have never left me to struggle alone. All the years of my life, You have been there to help me carry any burden I must bear, whether it is physical, emotional, or spiritual. I call out to You and You answer, just as my mother always did. She knew my voice and could pick my cry out from a babble of voices; You know my heart. When I cry out to You, You are there, just behind my shoulder, ready to catch me if I fall, ready to support me if I stagger. When my strength fails, Yours is always sufficient. Thank You for Your constant love and care, for picking out my cry and never failing to rescue me.

Day 348
Accepting the Gift

And I will pray the Father, and he shall give you another Comforter, that he may abide with you for ever.... I will not leave you comfortless: I will come to you.
JOHN 14:16, 18

Lord, You know that sometimes I reject Your promises. When I am really lonely and depressed, nothing seems to make me feel better. I know You are with me, I know You care when no one else cares—but some days even that is not enough. The fault is in me, not in You. On days like that, remind me that although Your promises are free for the taking, I still need to accept them, to claim them, and then to live in faith that they are mine. No gift is truly ours until we open it and accept it in thankfulness and joy.

Day 349
Riches Have Wings

Labour not to be rich: cease from thine own wisdom. Wilt thou set thine eyes upon that which is not? for riches certainly make themselves wings; they fly away as an eagle toward heaven.
PROVERBS 23:4–5

Over the years I have learned much about riches—in principle. I have learned that every time I save up a little, the roof will begin to leak or the driveway will need repaving. As soon as I make vacation plans and pay the nonrefundable deposit, one of us will not be able to get that week off. I've gotten used to this, Lord; I know how to roll with the punches. There will be other vacations, other Christmases. I am not seeking riches, anyway. Thank You for what I do have, which is happiness. Help me to be wise with what money I have and use it in a way that pleases You.

Day 350
Avoiding Sin

Neither yield ye your members as instruments of unrighteousness unto sin: but yield yourselves unto God, as those that are alive from the dead, and your members as instruments of righteousness unto God. For sin shall not have dominion over you: for ye are not under the law, but under grace.

ROMANS 6:13–14

The fight against sin is a serious struggle, Lord, one I face every day. Thank You for promising that as I wage war against sin, I am not under its dominion. Your grace frees me from my enemy, giving me the ability to be successful. I can choose not to follow Satan and to yield myself to Your will.

When Satan tempts me, pour out Your grace on me. Hold me firm in Your grasp, and empower me to do Your will. This battle can only be won in Your name.

Day 351
Blessings of Wisdom

For God giveth to a man that is good in his sight wisdom, and knowledge, and joy.
ECCLESIASTES 2:26

When I came to You, Lord, I expected forgiveness for my sins, but You have offered so much more! Not only do You give me the freedom from wrongdoing that I was seeking, You also give me three wonderful ways to live well and glorify You. Thank You for Your wisdom, thank You for the knowledge of how to live in Your sight, and thank You for the joy that floods my soul. Wisdom, knowledge, and joy are the "bumper crop" that accompanies forgiveness, an unexpected blessing to my soul. Your generous gifts are beyond compare.

Teach me to live in Your wisdom, knowledge, and joy. May they bless me, my family, and even the entire world around me.

Day 352
Founded on a Rock

Therefore whosoever heareth these sayings of mine, and doeth them, I will liken him unto a wise man, which built his house upon a rock: and the rain descended, and the floods came, and the winds blew, and beat upon that house; and it fell not: for it was founded upon a rock.
Matthew 7:24–25

All of us build our lives on something or around something—money, family, truth, love, even fear. Most of the time, my foundation is buried under the soil, where it is not seen by others; but it is still there, grounding my life and actions. Often my foundation is undependable and can send my life tumbling down after one bad storm. Teach me to ground my life on You, Lord, the only Rock who will stand forever against any storm.

Day 353
All-Powerful God

Have you never heard? Have you never understood? The LORD is the everlasting God, the Creator of all the earth. He never grows weak or weary. No one can measure the depths of his understanding.
ISAIAH 40:28 NLT

It's so easy for me to become tired of this world, Lord. When sin weighs me down or I can't understand this planet I live on, the burden seems almost unbearable. How glad I am that You, my omnipotent, powerful God, never feel that way. There's nothing You can't understand or overcome. You never have to rest because You will never face something stronger than Yourself.

I'm glad I can trust in You, Lord, to reach even the ends of the earth with Your power and authority. You control all things, wicked and blessed, and bend them to Your will. Thank You for all You do for this world—and for me.

Day 354
A Family

*For whosoever shall do the will of
my Father which is in heaven, the same
is my brother, and sister, and mother.*
MATTHEW 12:50

How amazing to think that You gave me a whole new family, Lord, when I didn't even think I needed one. But best of all, You gave me Yourself as an older brother, to guide me, watch out for me, and show me the best way to live.

I'm stunned to think You wanted me for Your sibling. How could You be proud of one who's so much smaller and weaker than You? Yet I am so thankful You chose me to live in Your eternal family.

Help me treat others in Your family as real brothers and sisters who share in You. I don't want any child in Your family to feel anything but loved.

Day 355
God's Strength

"The joy of the LORD is your strength."
NEHEMIAH 8:10 NKJV

I know I'm not much in my own power, Lord. Even at my strongest, life can turn me inside out in a moment, whether it's physically or spiritually. It doesn't take a lot to humble me.

But in You I can rejoice instead of worrying about my limitations. As I tap into Your power and authority, the challenges lessen. Instead of spending my time worrying about a problem, I can sing Your praises and share my faith in You. As my focus shifts from myself to You, Your joy fills my heart.

Thank You, Jesus, for being my strength. I rejoice in Your love and care for me.

Day 356
A Patient Spirit

*The end of a thing is better than its
beginning; the patient in spirit is
better than the proud in spirit.*

ECCLESIASTES 7:8 NKJV

I've been proud, Lord, so I understand what
You're talking about here. At times that old
haughty spirit still tempts me. I want things my
way, and I don't want to wait for Your better
path.

But You didn't leave me to my own desires.
You're working in me, slowly but surely, to turn
that pride into forbearance. You're strengthen-
ing my "patience muscles" as I grow in faith.

In the end, I will be better than I was on the
first day I came to You. The proud spirit that
once indwelled me has turned soft and gentle—
but strong. I'd never have done that under my
own power. Thank You for Your Spirit's work in
my heart.

Day 357
Take Water and Drink It

But whosoever drinketh of the water that I shall give him shall never thirst; but the water that I shall give him shall be in him a well of water springing up into everlasting life.
JOHN 4:14

Heavenly Father, I saw a sign warning hikers going down into the Grand Canyon to take water and drink it. I was surprised at the second part of the warning. But park rangers have found people unconscious from dehydration who were carrying full canteens. They had the water they needed to preserve their lives, but they failed to drink it.

Lord Jesus, I am blessed to have so many ways to learn about Your will. Yet, unless I make the effort to drink in Your Word, I am lost. The Bible says You, Lord Jesus, are the source of water that quenches spiritual thirst. Thank You for granting to me the water that brings life everlasting.

Day 358
Winter

Thou hast set all the borders of the earth:
thou hast made summer and winter.
PSALM 74:17

When I think of the words of the winter holiday season—candles, candy, carols, bows, and gifts—the weather doesn't seem as cold. The bother of shoveling snow disappears when I watch children make snow angels. The coldest season is in some ways the warmest one. It is difficult for me to give someone the cold shoulder when I hear the sounds of "Joy to the World."

Father, during the winter months, let me be friendly and bring warmth to others despite the freezing weather outside. May I greet strangers with a smile so sunny that it makes them feel less of a need for a heavy coat.

Day 359
Mary's Song of Praise

And Mary said, My soul doth magnify the Lord, and my spirit hath rejoiced in God my Saviour. For he hath regarded the low estate of his handmaiden: for, behold, from henceforth all generations shall call me blessed.

LUKE 1:46–48

Of all the women in the world—young or old, poor or rich, of high status or low—You chose a young girl from an unimportant, backwater province to bear Your Son, our Savior. Her response was, appropriately, a song of joy and praise, one of the most moving prayers in the Bible. Mary understood that You had given her a great honor that would be remembered forever, and she welcomed it—as well as the responsibility that came with it—with joy.

You bless my life in many ways every day, Father. May I receive Your blessings with a song of thanksgiving on my lips.

Day 360
Supplication

Be careful for nothing; but in every thing by
prayer and supplication with thanksgiving let
your requests be made known unto God.
PHILIPPIANS 4:6

Father, I am aware of many people who are suffering and who are in difficult situations. I pray that they and their families will be able to work out the difficulty. Help me to find a way to ease their burden.

I pray also for those people who live lives of quiet desperation—those who never reveal their distress but suffer in silent hopelessness. I pray that I will be sensitive to these individuals, recognize their concerns, and take action to relieve them of the suffering they are trying to bear by themselves.

Day 361
Clothed in Righteousness

Because thou sayest, I am rich, and increased with goods, and have need of nothing; and knowest not that thou art wretched, and miserable, and poor, and blind, and naked.

REVELATION 3:17

Heavenly Father, although I do not think of myself as rich, I have always had a home, food, and clothing. I recognize my happy circumstances when I think of those prophets of old who had stones for their pillows.

More important are the spiritual riches You give me. At one time I was walking in darkness, starved for love and unprotected from Satan. Now I am sheltered in Your love, nourished by Your Word, and clothed in the protection of the Holy Spirit. I love You, Lord, and will always be mindful of the rich blessings that fall on me.

Day 362
Attacking Problems

The Lord will rescue me from every
evil attack and will bring me safely
to his heavenly kingdom.
2 TIMOTHY 4:18 NIV

Lord, sometimes I look at problems out of the corner of my eye and pretend they are not there. I choose to ignore them, and they grow more serious because of my inattention. Whether they are big or small, I pray that I will accept challenges with a willing heart that will give me a greater chance of success. Help me attack problems before they attack me.

At times, it appears victory is a tiny island in a vast sea of trials. Sometimes I fail, but help me accept failure as an opportunity to try again with more experience. I pray that I will achieve worthy goals while changing for the better.

Day 363
Preaching to the Nations

*And this gospel of the kingdom shall be
preached in all the world for a witness unto
all nations; and then shall the end come.*
MATTHEW 24:14

Thank You, Lord, that You cared not just about
a few people, but that You sent the Gospel
message to the entire world. If You hadn't, I
might never have heard Your truth or come to
know You.

As missionaries seek to bring the Gospel into
the entire world, I ask Your blessing on them.
May their witness be a bright one that clearly
reflects Your love. Be with them in their trials
and joys, and increase Your witness to every
nation. May their testimony remain constantly
faithful to You until the end comes.

Day 364
Peaceful Harvest

And those who are peacemakers will plant seeds of peace and reap a harvest of righteousness.
JAMES 3:18 NLT

Lord, when I try to make peace with others in my world, I often think of the blessings of not having arguments, problems, and unresolved issues. I can't say I really look at the big picture, when just having the immediate blessing seems so good. But You promise me that as I make peace with friends, family, and coworkers, I will reap something else—righteousness.

I'm thankful that Your blessings are not small ones. As I obey You for the little things, You often give me an extra, even better blessing. Thank You for Your generosity. With this second harvest, I want to do good for others as well as myself.

Day 365
Answered Prayer

"And whatever things you ask in prayer,
believing, you will receive."
MATTHEW 21:22 NKJV

What a tremendous promise this is, Lord. As
You open heaven's treasures to me in these few
words, I see exactly how much You love me.

I know I can't take advantage of Your love,
Lord. Like a good earthly father, You never
allow me to have anything that would really
harm me, no matter how much I demand it. But
as my faith grows, I begin to ask for things that
benefit Your kingdom instead of fulfilling my
greed. The more I know You, the more I pray in
Your will, and the more You answer with a "yes."

Help me to ask for the right things, Lord,
and give me faith to believe You'll provide them.
Then when I receive my answer, we'll both be
blessed.

Scripture Index

Daily Inspiration for a Woman's Spirit!

Daily Encouragement: 3-Minute Devotions for Women

This delightful daily devotional packs a powerful dose of comfort, encouragement, and joy into just-right-sized readings for women of all ages.

Paperback / 978-1-64352-505-1 / $9.99

Pray through the Bible in a Year Devotional

This beautiful daily devotional features a plan for reading through the Bible in a year with an accompanying prayer inspired by that day's scripture reading—just for you.

Paperback / 978-1-64352-727-7 / $9.99